Heidegger's Hut

Heidegger's Hut

The MIT Press   Cambridge, Massachusetts   London, England

Adam Sharr including photographs by Digne Meller-Marcovicz

First MIT Press new paperback edition, 2017

© 2006 Massachusetts Institute of Technology

Except as noted in the captions, all illustrations in this book © 2006 Adam Sharr.

This book was set in Minion and Syntax by Graphic Composition, Inc., and was printed and bound in the United States of America.

Library of Congress Cataloging-in-Publication Data

Sharr, Adam.
    Heidegger's hut / Adam Sharr ; includes photographs by Digne Meller-Marcovicz.
        p. cm.
    Includes bibliographical references (p.   ) and index.
    ISBN-13: 978-0-262-19551-5 (hc.: alk. paper)
    ISBN-13: 978-0-262-53366-9 (pb.: alk. paper)
    1. Heidegger, Martin, 1889–1976—Homes and haunts—Germany—Todtnauberg. I. Title.

    B3279.H49S425 2006
    193—dc22

                                                                        2006043834

10 9 8 7 6 5 4

To Chris and Colin Sharr

CONTENTS

Is the hut described in this text the smallest residence ever to merit a monograph? Might it be the most prosaic, too? Adam Sharr's text is accordingly concise and direct, and this foreword will not unbalance the arrangement. It aims instead to anticipate what readers might ask before deciding whether to read this book. For instance: Is this really a book about a hut? Yes, and no. This is the most thorough architectural "crit" of a hut ever set down, the justification for which is that the hut was the setting in which Martin Heidegger wrote phenomenological texts that became touchstones for late-twentieth-century architectural theory. Sharr accepts that his own training is as an architect, not as a philosopher. His slim volume contains no explicit philosophical treatise, then, nor any overt statement of theoretical position, but instead invites architects to do some thinking induced by philosophy, and philosophers to some thinking prompted by architecture.

Sharr revisits Heidegger's phenomenology with a detailed, empirical description of the phenomena that were before the eyes of the phenomenologist. In doing this Sharr does not discover some lost truth behind Heidegger's allusive writing, though the book will likely startle readers in the way it "grounds" the Heideggerian theory of grounding: rather than simply claim a connection between place and being, why not investigate the association by aligning the sites and ideas of Heidegger's own life? While mindful that dwelling is not crudely interchangeable with physical occupation, Sharr's scrupulous attention to material fact and anthropological record pursues a valid inquiry. Building, dwelling, and thinking are, after all, empirical problems—pragmatic, temporal, spatial, and material—so it seems to be a matter of more than prying interest to inquire how

Heidegger himself went about them. And while Heidegger explicitly rejected the conversion of his philosophy into an architectural manual, he held up his life at Todtnauberg as a high ideal.

This book also presents an opportunity to compare Heidegger's own spatial practice with the influential architectural pedagogy informed by his thought (for example through Christian Norberg-Schulz, beginning in the 1960s). That comparison may yet expose a mismatch of actuality and methodology, or initiate a more faithfully "Heideggerian" architectural practice. In the interim, Sharr's book demonstrates a distinctive architectural competence. Contemporary architecture has a tendency to find the practical competences at its core somewhat humdrum; this book gives something back to the intellectual commonwealth precisely by its careful, unassuming articulation of architectural knowledge—its inventory of the pieces of Heidegger's modest houses, and of the spatial relationships of his life. In this the book conciliates between those architects drawn to theory and those avowedly led by practice.

This book is not, in the end, a textual pilgrimage to Todtnauberg. Sharr visits Heidegger's hut as a political liberal, and possibly as something of an architectural agnostic. Built in 1922 and unascribed, Heidegger's hut is unexceptional at one level, Sharr admits and shows, and the philosopher's domestic arrangements prove to have had a bourgeois predictability. What takes Sharr to Todtnauberg is a curiosity about Heidegger's program to quell the anxiety of existence by giving the subject physical and temporal certainties. The same essentialism could and can be pathological, and while Sharr concurs with the general consensus that Heideggerianism has a profound validity outside the extreme right, it would be disingenuous to emphasize the relationships only between Todtnauberg and Heidegger's *good* intentions.

Consideration of this hut and the thoughts that occurred here is a potentially misguided enterprise, then. Why risk it? For those who read Heidegger's philosophy, the spatial biography contained in this book will be of inherent interest, though this alone would not justify the book's appearance on the architectural bookshelf. This book will not contribute, either, to the architectural literature that apologizes for designs with unacceptable political pedigree on the basis of aesthetic interest. Architecturally, the principal matter on the minds of most contemporary readers will probably be this: Building and everyday life have been fundamentally altered by modernity, and Heidegger's work and the hut in which the work took place (and which is written into the work) have become figured as a point of resistance to modernization. In architectural theory, Heideggerianism has become somewhat secularized, recuperated from its turgid theology and nauseating political affiliations. Heidegger's identification of the crisis of dwelling, and his course of treatment for it, have been retained for an anti-technocratic discourse more cogently articulated by liberals than conservatives, though available to either.

Modernity occupies an ambiguous relationship within the programs of conservative and progressive politics alike. Nazism was itself represented by two iconographies, one medievalizing, the other mechanistic. If historically the leftist intelligentsia has mostly adopted modernization as a force for emancipation, it has also harbored serious reservations about modernization's disintegrative impact upon subjectivity and its violent destruction of habitat. No architect in the twenty-first century is immune to the contradictions of modernity and its successor, postmodernity, so Heidegger remains a component in the canon of architectural theory, even where he serves as a dialectical opposite, as he does for posthumanists and poststructuralists.

Though Heidegger's hut might seem an absurd place in which to ride out the tempest of modernization, many intellectuals and architects will find it difficult to disavow any curiosity about this place. If, as Heidegger claimed, technology has made us at home everywhere and nowhere, a rooftop antenna the sign that we are not in fact at home, the level of detail Sharr assembles here matters. Heidegger's eventual capitulation to telephone and electricity, which might otherwise pass as a petty detail and a sensible convenience to an old man, comes as a rude interruption to the purity of the Todtnauberg project. Sharr presents us with a beguilingly realistic portrayal of an originary trope of architectural aesthetics, the hut—the supposed domicile of the hermit, the philosopher, and primitivism. Sharr presents us not with the arboreal framework of an eighteenth-century print, but with a place used by a modern intellectual and his entourage, no less iconic to twentieth-century philosophy than Wittgenstein's empty white office at Cambridge University. Philosophy, though the discipline is often reluctant to admit to the fact, is an embodied process that takes place in buildings and prompts thoughts about the ideal arrangement of space. Readers of this book may very well empathize with Heidegger's determination to retreat from his suburban house, hike off the grid, and complete thoughts to the accompaniment of the sound of a spring and changes in the direction of the clouds. This empathy will likely be accompanied by a slight discomfort, attributable in part to the withering since the 1960s of the intellectual and political credibility of dropping out, in part to the underlying paradox that intellectual production—an industry embedded in the communications nexus—is carried out in spaces modeled on the premodern typologies of hut and monastic cell.

The thinking of the Frankfurt school on the one hand and of Heidegger's school on the other continue to define two forms of modern truth: the one discovered, through work in the metropolitan library and urban loft, by the dialectic of ideal and real, the other revealed by an encounter with an uncorrupted ideal at the rural retreat. Nevertheless, the opposition between metropolis and province which underpins both Heidegger's philosophy and the theories that contest it is easily overstated. Though much criticism has been rightly directed at the vain exclusion of the Other by Heidegger's *domus,* the metropolis has its own silently violent separations, which presently employ market mechanisms, methods of display, and policing to spirit away socio-aesthetic interruptions to the bright tableaux vivantes of the metropolitan ideal. Metropolitan loft and rustic hut (with their comparably bold economies of architectural form) meanwhile concur in their repulsion by mediocrity, their rejection of vulgar rationalization, and their remove from manual labor, collectivism, and family life, and thus they jointly provide the existential footholds from which architectural theory has attempted to identify the values with which to build. Indeed, heroic encounters with midtown Manhattan and Todtnauberg have more in common with each other than they do with those landscapes more usually passing as urban and rural—with sprawl and agrarian expanse, where an architect is more than ever faced with the unlikelihood of realizing the sense of dwelling.

Yet the practices of living, inhabiting, and thinking go on, and must take place somewhere. Sharr allows us a brief insight into his own approach to this problem as an architect (which takes place alongside his scholarship). He asks us:

Why cannot every life hold out hope for a resonant, centering datum? This need not keep others at bay, cast them as strangers, or be situated outside the city. The hut's memory suggests strategies for making such a datum. It might frame in rich and multiple ways itself, its inhabitants and their relationships, its equipment, its social context, the theater of passersby, the sun and tracking shadows, glimpses of the sky, breeze and wind, rain and snow, flora and fauna. It might be neither too big nor unnecessarily flexible, instead helping its occupants to configure intensities of situation. It might encourage reflective moments thought at a slower pace. Configuring daily, weekly, and seasonal routines, such a datum could dignify and sustain any life, attuned to the commonplace closely watched.

It seems a somewhat anodyne appeal: to restore a sense of place, boundary, tectonics, materiality, and social relations; to *present* the world rather than *represent* it. The call will be familiar, in fact, to advocates of critical regionalism, itself inspired in part by readings of Heidegger. Its modesty is, nonetheless, Sharr's probable project. The first architect to dare venture into the hut itself, he less canonizes it than demystifies it. Unable to precisely attribute the hut's design to Heidegger himself, Sharr does not even allow the hut to serve as the ultimate model for "Heideggerian" architecture. He readily allows that Heidegger's politics were an abomination but by default requires the reader to concede that any belief in something at Todtnauberg conducive to political crime would itself be essentialist. In the remoteness of Todtnauberg, Sharr notes a distanced psychological relationship between Heidegger and others (and the Other) and responds as an architect, aware that remoteness will not be a component of better buildings in the twenty-first century.

At the conclusion of a memorable intellectual and aesthetic hike around the Todtnauberg hut and the still more vivid architectural analogies written there, Sharr finds only one, diffident reason for having made the journey, regardless of what others may make of it: to improve the day-to-day experience of living through a pragmatic relationship between architectural theory and architecture practice. Sharr hopes to heighten everyday experiences of architecture even prior to the occupants' true deliverance by, or from, modernity. This improvement, Sharr implies, remains the assignment of thinking architects.

Simon Sadler

Heidegger's actual hut at Todtnauberg is as much a philosophical event as it is an
architectural one. Opened up in both instances are sites of activity. The activity in
question centers on the question of how "place" is to be understood. With place there
arises the complex relationship not just between philosophy and geography but also, and
just as acutely, between geography and creativity. Even though when first posed it appears
to be a simplistic question, nonetheless it is possible to ask what type of relationship exists
between geography—understood as the place of writing—and that act which brings
writing and thinking together. This is not an act in any abstract sense. Rather it is one
with a particular orientation, if not mode of expression. It is possible to suggest, for
example—even if the prompt guiding such a suggestion would need to be questioned—
that the setting of Delphi in Greece, its actual physical position, with the siting of the
Temple of Apollo on the side of Mount Parnassus, adds more force to the Heraclitean
fragment that begins with the evocation of the Delphic oracle.[1] Would such a positioning
have exhibited any hold if the oracle were to have been found in a back street in Piraeus?
No matter how amusing such a suggestion may be—and it could even be precisely
because it is amusing—what it gestures toward is a type of truth. Namely, the apparent
implausibility of the oracle being so located already suggests that there is a type of
relationship between place and forms of thought. Place, once given a more precise
delimitation, needs to be defined in terms of specific positions.

For the major part of his writing life, Heidegger wrote in two locations, the house
on Rötebuckweg in Freiburg and the hut at Todtnauberg. The former is a location in the
city, a site uncelebrated, rarely functioning as a place of pilgrimage. Celan and Derrida

traveled to Todtnauberg. For Celan the visit occasioned one of his most exacting poems. Heidegger knew he had to work in the university, research in a library, write in the city. And yet a question that cannot be escaped concerns the compatibility between a certain mode of thinking and the urban condition. The question insists precisely because these places did not define his work. The urban as condition, for Heidegger, stands at an important distance from the hut. The hut is both a place and an emblem for a type of philosophical practice. Procedurally, however, a way in is needed. The hut has to be approached. This is the case because the hut should not be understood as though the philosophical had to be identified with the rural; that would be to misunderstand Heidegger's commitment to the hut and to what it afforded. The urban and the provincial in terms of everyday life are potentially imbricated (living in town, holidaying in the country, etc.).[2] In terms of the relations between thinking and place, the forced intrusion of the everyday, for Heidegger, will not pertain. Hence the hut's emblematic presence.

Of the many ways into an understanding of the differences between the urban and the provincial (recognizing that the latter is Heidegger's own term), a productive one is provided by Walter Benjamin's *One Way Street*. As a book it consists of a series of short texts. Neither prose poems nor essays, they have both a style and a content of their own. In *One Way Street,* Benjamin locates the city dweller's sense of location and place in the following terms:

Freiburg Minster.—The special sense of a town [*dem eigensten Heimatgefühl einer Stadt*] is formed in part for its inhabitants—and perhaps even in the memory of a traveller who has stayed there—by the tone and intervals with which its tower clock begins to chime.[3]

The force of this evocation of the tower clock is that place and time come to define urban being. The time in question—its positioning in relation to memory—is defined by the clock. The question raised by the description concerns the relationship between this conception of time—the complex interplay of what in the end is chronological time and the pulse of a city—and another, perhaps more primordial sense of time. Formulated in these terms, a distinction is introduced: Either a differentiation between the primordial and the temporality implicit in the interplay of memory and the urban pulse is no more than a mystification, or on the contrary its philosophical acuity generates a different sense of project. The insistence of the primordial—and therefore the need to insist on it—would be the necessity to think its essential differentiation from embodied and lived temporalities. It is of course at this precise point that Heidegger's hut enters upon the scene. Embodied and lived temporalities bring specific conceptions of place into play. Place defined by the urban and thus the city carry and are carried by such a conception of time. Moreover, they allow for the possibility that with the urban the body, as a locus of time and place, is central. Counterposed to this possibility is the hut. This counterposition places the hut, and thereby opens up the hut as a place. (And with that opening up—in the very distinction that there would be between Heidegger and Benjamin—there is the need to think what a counterpositioning in both architecture and philosophy would be like.)

Note, however, that this opposition is not simply one between the city and the countryside. At stake here are two distinct philosophical possibilities. The first would eschew a concern with the primordiality of either time or being. The second would demand it. The hut comes to the fore within a philosophical project that conceives of time and being in this latter sense. It is their primordiality that makes the question of geography—thus place—other than one situated within a simple opposition city/country. Equally, the sense of dwelling in both instances cannot be understood in terms of these simple oppositions.

What then of the hut, the place that many take as demonstrating Heidegger's commitment to the provincial? The force of Adam Sharr's study is that it allows access to this question in a way that resists any easy slide into identifying Heidegger with simple provinciality or seeing the celebration of the urban as its straightforward opposite. If there is a way of situating Heidegger's hut as a philosophical as well as an architectural event, it has to be grounded not just in a conception of time and being as admitting an inherent primordiality but in the possibility that such a conception be allowed to hold sway. (The latter is a possibility having a lived and thus placed dimension.) That can occur to the extent that a relationship to place is neither instrumentalized nor made monolithic. In regard to the latter, Heidegger asserts that landscape is not reduced for him to the object of observation—landscape as an aesthetic event. Almost in the guise of autobiography he notes, "Strictly speaking I myself never observe the landscape. I experience its hourly changes, day and night, in the great comings and goings of the seasons." This passage, quoted by Sharr, is central to any understanding of the relationship between the placedness of the hut and Heidegger's philosophical project.

Worked through Heidegger's own philosophical writings, this passage reflects those moments in which a notion of freedom is advocated. Not the freedom identified by Schelling, let alone the conception of freedom that is articulated within the writings of traditional political philosophy; rather, this conception of freedom involves the letting appear—or letting be—of that which is there most fundamentally. (As will be noted, it is this structure that brings the distinction between the authentic and the inauthentic into play.) This letting appear emerges with real clarity in Heidegger's own treatment of the distinction between the "ready to hand" and the "present to hand" in *Being and Time*.[4] Moreover, it is a positioning that is reflected throughout his writings up to the conception of *Gelassenheit* in the later works.[5]

At stake in instances of this nature is the claim that, independently of a possible aestheticization of objects or their individuation within an economy of utility, there is an ineliminable connectedness such that what may—the "may" of "potentiality"—come to the fore is the original relation. That originality cannot be imposed as though a founding state of affairs could be re-presented to that which is being considered, like a type of framing mechanism. Nor, moreover, can it be simply, and thus passively, awaited. There needs to be a philosophical positioning that, while allowing for an original state of affairs—whether it is the primordiality of Being or an original state of connectedness with the world—has to be allowed to appear. This will be an appearing that works beyond the hold of mere passivity or action (if the latter is understood instrumentally). Distancing both activity and passivity, in the case of *Dasein,* is defined by Heidegger in terms of "potentiality." *Being and Time* presents this position in the following way:

Dasein is an entity for which in its Being, that Being is an issue. The phrase "is an issue" has been made plain in the state-of-Being of understanding—of understanding as self-projective

Being towards its ownmost potentiality-for-Being. This potentiality is that for the sake of which any Dasein is as it is. In each case Dasein has already compared itself, in its Being, with a possibility of itself. Being-free for one's ownmost potentiality for Being, and therewith for the possibility of authenticity and inauthenticity is shown with a primordial elemental concreteness, in anxiety.[6]

By "anxiety" Heidegger refers to an elemental way of being in the world and thus signals on the level of a determining mood the original relation between *Dasein* and world. What is significant about this passage is the relationship between *Dasein*'s own possibility and that state of Being-free for the realization of that state of affairs. What is positioned therefore is openness emerging within a structure of philosophical necessity. (This necessity arises because the relationship between potentiality and Being-free is part of a definition of the ontological character of human being.) Heidegger situates this openness neither in the city nor the country. It is situated—in terms of a lived encounter with the actuality of this potentiality—within a setting in which what is present is not already positioned in terms of an aesthetic or instrumental determination. Heidegger finds this possibility in the "provinces"—in his hut.

Note therefore that the hut, rather than involving a merely literal commitment to the countryside or the provinces, involves a commitment to a particular relationship between philosophy and place. The particularity in question is not a mere geographical location. Rather, it is the way the philosophical is understood and thus the reciprocal relation that such an understanding has to place. (It could be that the same "place" would be understood differently if there were another conception of the philosophical at work.) It is not just that both are related; they are defined or conceived in terms of each other. Hence, when Walter Benjamin evokes Freiburg or Naples (to name but two of the cities that appear in his writings), these places emerge within a conception of philosophical activity on the one hand, and a particular conception of the relationship between place and the way the task of writing unfolds on the other.

In architectural terms there cannot be any naivety in relation to the hut. The architectural position mirrors the philosophical one. Adam Sharr has provided an invaluable resource in presenting the history of the hut and, more importantly, images as well as models of it. What to make of the hut within such a presentation remains an open question. Sharr's own conclusion is that the hut for Heidegger provided the possibility for a specific type of philosophical work. Philosophy and place (here the hut in its broadest sense) oriented each other. As such, it can be concluded that there is an important link between geography (place) and modes of thinking. Sharr recognizes that this connection may have opened up paths for Heidegger that will no longer be followed. Nonetheless we need to think how that relationship is to be understood. If there is a complex relationship between the hut and that which was thought philosophically, will a critique of the philosophical position necessitate abandoning the hut in the name of another place (and thus another conception of place with other architectural possibilities)? There is, of course, the reciprocal question: Will an architectural critique necessitate the adoption—though it may be the case that the effectiveness of the critique will signal its already having been adopted—of another philosophical position? The value of Adam Sharr's work is that it allows both of these questions to be pursued while at the same time providing an invaluable architectural and philosophical resource.

Andrew Benjamin

NOTE

Heidegger's house on Rötebuckweg, Freiburg-im-Breisgau, is in private ownership. The residents have requested the addition of a note to this book asking potential visitors to respect their privacy.

Heidegger's hut at Todtnauberg also remains private property. The following text is printed on a tourist sign recently sited near the building with the heading "Why the hut is not a museum": "Martin Heidegger has two sons, fourteen grandchildren and, by 2002, had twenty-one great-grandchildren. The hut is still owned by the Heidegger family and used privately by them. Visitors are not permitted. Please respect the privacy of the family."

ACKNOWLEDGMENTS

This text has origins in a doctoral dissertation submitted to the Welsh School of Architecture in Cardiff, who supported my research with a studentship and travel grant. Simon Unwin was a wise and thoughtful supervisor of that dissertation. Its examiners, Andrew Ballantyne and Flora Samuel, helped with development. Gertrud Heidegger and Fr. Heinrich Heidegger kindly gave their time and offered many insights. Mark Giles interpreted (and drove). Prof. Dr. Hugo Ott forwarded material on Heidegger's Freiburg house. Contributions were made by friends, colleagues, critics, and readers in the cities— Cardiff, London, Nottingham, and Cardiff again—where this book was written: Andy Carr, Nader El-Bizri, Sally Fry, Ed Green, Jonathan Hale, Jonathan Harwood, Patrick Hannay, Dean Hawkes, Gisela Löhlein, Rhiannon Mason, Jo Odgers, Simon Sadler, Paola Sassi, Bernhard Schmid, Nicholas Temple, Richard Weston, Clare and Sandy Wright. My architectural clients, particularly David Clarke, Lucy McCall, and Mary and Michael Elster, have indulged attempts to confront problems in building raised by this book. I've benefited from the careful guidance of Roger Conover at the MIT Press, and I'm indebted to the Press's anonymous referees, especially one whose incisive comments on two drafts are appreciated. This book would not have been finished without Joanne Sayner, whose support, criticism, and generous morality have kept me on an even course. Chris and Colin Sharr have offered patient and friendly encouragement for over three decades.

Adam Sharr
Plasnewydd, Cardiff, September 2005

Heidegger's Hut

1. Heidegger's hut at
Todtnauberg.

INTRODUCTION

This book is about an intense relationship between place and person. In summer 1922, Martin Heidegger (1889–1976) moved into a small cabin built for him high in the Black Forest mountains of southern Germany (fig. 1). Heidegger called this building, approximately six meters by seven, "die Hütte" ("the hut"). He worked on many of his most famous writings there, from early lectures that bewitched students and began to shape the book *Being and Time* to his last and arguably most enigmatic texts. Heidegger thought and wrote at the hut over five decades, often alone, claiming an emotional and intellectual intimacy with the building, its surroundings, and its seasons.

To Heidegger, Todtnauberg was more than a physical location. In 1934, he spoke of taking in his philosophical work as a part of the mountains, the work finding him at one with the landscape.[1] He located himself as a susceptible scribe, suggesting that philosophy suspended the landscape in words through him almost without agency. The philosopher claimed a poignant sustenance in the changing climate of the locality, the building's sense of interiority, the distant view of the Alps, and the spring alongside. He attributed a "hidden law" to the philosophy of the mountains.[2] While some have found value in the thinking of Heidegger's provincialism, others find troubling his abdication of agency and tendency to romanticism, given his prominent involvement with the Nazi regime in 1930s Germany. In approaching Heidegger's writings—notably those about "dwelling" and "place" that have interested architects—it is important to consider the circumstances in which the philosopher felt "transported" into the work's "own rhythm."[3]

This book aims to describe and present Heidegger's hut to help readers with their interpretations of that small building. No detailed account of it has been published before. The hut's configuration is recorded here, along with its location, how it came to be built, the layout of its three rooms, and how it was used. The discussion draws from original material, including interviews with the philosopher's relatives. It refers to Heidegger's accounts of how he perceived the hut and some accounts of visitors to Todtnauberg. The book also describes another building that was a key part of Heidegger's life and which helps to clarify his involvement with the hut: a suburban house built for him and his family on the edge of Freiburg-im-Breisgau, some thirty kilometers away and a thousand meters below. The lack of feeling evident in Heidegger's writings for this suburban existence helps to clarify aspects of the resonance he found in mountain life.

Heidegger was born on 26 September 1889 into a provincial, lower-middle-class family in Meßkirch, an agrarian town in Heuberg near the edge of the Black Forest. His father was a barrel-maker and church sexton, his mother a housewife. The family's orthodox Catholicism ran deep, their particular faith a central plank of their identity in the context of Protestant state institutions and a dominant local "Old Catholic" minority.[4] Through his family, the young Heidegger became deeply involved in the church. His education, initially toward the priesthood, was funded by grants held in its gift. He turned to academic study of theology and philosophy after a brief and unsuccessful enrollment at a Jesuit institution.[5] In 1917, during a period of First World War army service in the meteorological corps, he married Elfride Petri, a student of economics from Prussia. Sons were born to the couple in 1919 and 1920. After the war, Heidegger taught at his alma mater, the Albert-Ludwig University of Freiburg, as assistant to the eminent philosopher Edmund Husserl.[6] At this time, he began to distance himself from the philosophy of religion and the practice of Catholicism, seemingly finding them an encumbrance to his aspirations toward the philosophical elite. Heidegger was appointed to a chair of philosophy at Marburg University from 1923, around the time of the hut's construction, returning to Freiburg to succeed Husserl upon his retirement in 1928. This post was secured on the strength of *Being and Time*, a text intended as part of a larger work, published in the previous year and largely written at Todtnauberg—a place which by this time had become deeply significant for him.

Largely due to the international acclaim of *Being and Time,* Heidegger had become something of a public figure by the early 1930s. At this point, he abandoned attempts to complete that text within the original framework. He also began his controversial involvement with Nazism.[7] In April 1933, Heidegger took up the rectorship of Freiburg University amid political "restructuring."[8] He joined the Nazi party, helping to implement some of their academic policies and giving a number of lectures and speeches in which he mixed philosophical vocabulary with party propaganda.[9] He resigned his post as rector in April 1934, reputedly disillusioned with the regime, and returned to research and teaching.[10] Shortly after, he began to write *Contributions to Philosophy (From Enowning),* a series of reflections published posthumously in 1989, which some commentators now consider to be his most significant work.[11] According to Heidegger's contested postwar apologia, he spent the remaining Hitler years in quiet resistance of the regime.[12] Nevertheless, in 1946 the university found Heidegger to have put his academic reputation at the service of the Nazi party, validating it at a crucial time, and his teaching was judged too "unfree" for contemporary circumstances.[13] He was forcibly retired, pensioned, and prevented from teaching until further notice. The university senate relaxed their view in 1950 following petitions from Heidegger's sympathizers, and he was granted the status of emeritus professor in 1951, his teaching suspension formally lifted.[14] In later life, Heidegger wrote for publication and gave occasional lectures and seminars. He maintained near total silence about fascism and its brutal consequences. He worked into his final years but publications slowed. Heidegger died on 26 May 1976 in Freiburg and was buried in Meßkirch.

Heidegger felt that his own life was uninteresting with respect to his thought. However, tensions between his biography and philosophy appear particularly acute. Many struggle to reconcile this thinker, who asked questions of "being" so bewitchingly, with the professor figure painted by biographers who deployed his distinctive philosophical vocabulary in support of the Nazi regime. Yet the suggestion that philosophy transcends biography is problematic, and in Heidegger's case, to make this argument is arguably to become an apologist for the most troubling aspects of his writings. Any attempt at reconciliation of Heidegger's life with his work lies beyond the scope of this book. However, the philosopher's interpretations of the hut at Todtnauberg raise questions about provincialism that run through his work like a red thread.

While the romanticizing of country life is perceived in many cultures as the obscure and indulgent preserve of dreamers, the path of German romantic provincialism remains far more difficult. *Heimat* (dedication to home), region, nation, and language have here been distinctively aligned.[15] Some have argued that, into the twentieth century, a conjunction of writers such as Hölderlin, Herder, and Nietzsche helped to open up a *Sonderweg,* a special German path to Nazism, prefiguring Hitler and establishing an intellectual space to be invaded by his bloody rhetoric.[16] Whether such a path predestined fascism or is merely identifiable with the benefit of hindsight remains a question contested by historians. Whichever side one takes in this debate, the path of German romanticism looms large in Heidegger's writings before, during, and after Nazism.[17] Some find the conjunction of this inclination with the philosopher's Nazi involvement sufficient to invalidate his thinking, some simply take political exception to his work, while others choose to ignore Heidegger's politics and yet others try to align themselves between these polarities. In parallel, it is possible to follow many interpretations of Heidegger's hut: as the site of a heroic confrontation between philosopher and existence, as the petit bourgeois escape of a misguided romantic, as a place with fascist overtones that remains suspicious, or as an entirely unremarkable little building. It is not the intention of this book to promote one of these possibilities or any alternative; rather, I offer up for readers the hut itself and Heidegger's interpretations of it. In order to study Heidegger's work and that of philosophers and architects who have drawn from it, I think it is important to engage with the hut at Todtnauberg but to do so properly informed, critically and at an appropriate distance.

Through his writings on dwelling and place, especially the essays "Building Dwelling Thinking" and ". . . Poetically, Man Dwells . . . ," Heidegger's work became important to a number of canonical architects and architectural writers during the latter part of the twentieth century.[18] Architectural debate drew from particular aspects of Heidegger's writings that were deeply influenced by his mountain life—notably, an acknowledgment of place measured emotionally alongside space measured mathematically; a mythical view of a past building and dwelling once unified as a single activity, but now disrupted by professional procedures and technological processes; a desire for a meaningful temporal and physical order; a sensitivity toward dimensions of presence and absence; and a mutual intermediation of mind, body, and place. Responses to Heidegger were numerous, in writing from Christian Norberg-Schulz, Kenneth Frampton, Dalibor Vesely, and Alberto Pérez-Gómez, among others, and in building from Hans Scharoun, Christopher Alexander, Colin St. John Wilson, Steven Holl, Juhani Pallasmaa, and Peter Zumthor.[19] The study of Heidegger's hut at Todtnauberg not only helps to clarify his writings on dwelling and place but illuminates the responses of such commentators.

In 1966, Heidegger granted an interview to the German news magazine *Der Spiegel*, partly to rehearse his own account of his rectorship, on condition that the text should be printed only after his death.[20] At that time—and during a later visit in June 1968—accompanying photographs were taken of the philosopher at his Freiburg house and at the Todtnauberg hut by the young photojournalist Digne Meller-Marcovicz. Some of her images are used to illustrate this book. Aspects of these photographs, notably those at Todtnauberg, appear staged, such as the traditional regional garments chosen by Heidegger and his wife and some of the poses struck—the philosopher apparently engaged deep in thought, and the particular show of domesticity. Yet Meller-Marcovicz's photographs comprise a remarkable account of Heidegger's surroundings, offering a vivid portrait of his mountain life.

The hut remained a constant dialogue partner for Heidegger from 1922 onward. He seemed to feel most at home in this small building, which conditioned a milieu that sustained thinking for him. In the structure and the motions of its surrounding landscape can be seen reflected the circumstances of his work. The hut thus offers opportunities for considering his life and his writings, as well as challenges to his thought. The philosopher's life and work remain fundamentally enmeshed with the circumstances of his thinking. To properly engage with Heidegger's writings, it is necessary to engage in detail with his life at Todtnauberg and its conditions.

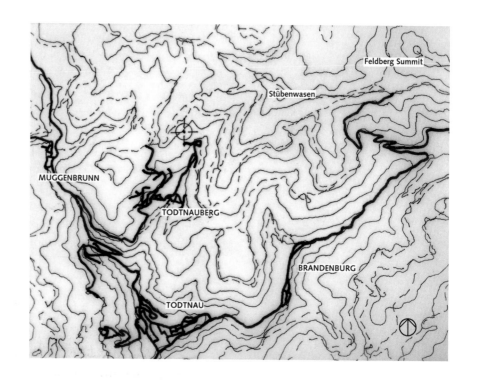

Feldberg Summit

Stübenwasen

MUGGENBRUNN

TODTNAUBERG

BRANDENBURG

TODTNAU

2. Map of Todtnauberg and its

surroundings.

Waters rising in the mountains of southwest Germany's *Hochschwarzwald*, the high Black Forest, find their way into two of Europe's longest rivers, the Rhine and the Danube. From north to south, this district runs from Freiburg-im-Breisgau, the capital of Baden, to the German-Swiss border. Views from its slopes survey the mountains of three countries, from the Vosges in France to the Swiss Alps. Most human settlement in this terrain is to be found in its valleys, which afford some respite from extremes of weather. The highlands are barely inhabited except for a few mountain *Hütten*—ski huts ranging from single-cell refuges to catered hostels—scattered across the terrain.

The tallest mountain in the *Hochschwarzwald* is Feldberg, rising 1,493 meters above mean sea level. A number of ridges radiate from the base of its peak. Walking and ski paths trace these ridges, their spurs descending into valleys beyond. Two routes from the Stübenwasen ridge descend to follow a V-shaped valley, converging at the village of Todtnauberg which lies in its bowl (fig. 2). A tree line encircles the top of this valley. Below is settlement and managed forestry containing a dense network of forest paths. The landscape above the trees is markedly different: bleaker, opening to distant horizons. Beyond the village, a path descends through the trees, following a waterfall to drop another five hundred meters over two kilometers to the town of Todtnau.

The local economy, once reliant on agriculture and forestry, now depends much upon ski tourism. The village of Todtnauberg has grown rapidly in consequence, and a collection of small hotels and apartments has spread along the valley in the last thirty years (figs. 3, 4). Despite much new building, the village's core is still dominated by a

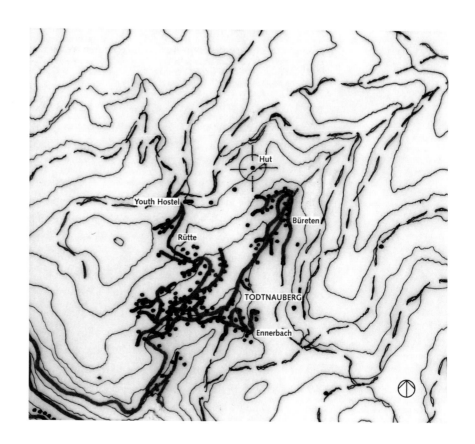

Labels on map:
Hut
Youth Hostel
Büreten
Rütte
TODTNAUBERG
Ennerbach

3. Map showing the hut and
the extent of Todtnauberg
village today.

number of eighteenth- and nineteenth-century timber-built *Schwarzwaldhöfe,* Black Forest farmhouses with high pitched roofs and low eaves.

At around 1,100 meters altitude, Todtnauberg is below the tree line but still within the mountain microclimate. Its rapidly changing weather patterns are striking, as high peaks and deep valleys create localized extremes of climate (fig. 5). When moisture levels prompt mists to rise, distant prospects are obscured. When rain sets in, views can be limited to a few hundred meters. In contrast to its expansive setting, the area then assumes a sense of introversion. Prospects can appear or disappear in minutes. The summer has hot sunshine, often interspersed with showers. Reemerging after rain, the sun lifts clouds of steam from trees and hills. In winter, a thick blanket of snow falls which remains long into spring on higher slopes; snow shaded by peculiarities of terrain can be found in early summer. Weather may also vary significantly between neighboring valleys. While there might be clear sunshine in one, rain has set in for the day at another— indeed, from certain points on higher paths, both may be seen at once. This meteorological drama can have an immediate impact upon life in the district.

Heidegger's hut is to be found in the valley above Todtnauberg on the edge of the forest (fig. 6). It lies one kilometer northeast of the village center and approximately one hundred meters higher, clearly identifiable as the building at which the philosopher was photographed in residence in 1968. Many texts exaggerate the hut's remoteness.[21] Although the small timber-clad building was reasonably distant from other structures when constructed, the village now stretches along the valley below. Half buried into the bank, the hut appears almost at one with the slope.

4. Todtnauberg from the apex of the valley, showing the extent of building there in 2005. Heidegger's hut is near the top of the valley, approximately central, but covered by trees from this viewpoint.

5. Clouds hanging in the valley after a storm. Heidegger's hut is at the right of this photograph near the top of the slope.

6. Heidegger's hut still looks
much as it did when Heidegger
was photographed there in
1968.

7. A small, steep path leads
downhill to the hut.

THE HUT IN THE VALLEY

Only one surfaced road reaches Todtnauberg, from Muggenbrunn on the Notschrei Pass between Freiburg and Todtnau. A fork of this road continues beyond the village to a youth hostel just below the valley's southern ridge. A number of marked walking and ski tracks diverge from this hostel into the forest, many rutted with deep tire marks when foresters are logging. One of these tracks leads to the hut. It descends a little, following the ridge. A fork curves back toward the village and skirts the tree line, allowing periodic glimpses across the valley. The hut is first revealed in one of these glimpses at a point where, in 2002, local authorities erected a tourist sign identifying the building. A little further on, at a small clearing, a path leads downhill to the back of the hut (fig. 7). This steep path remains the principal access to the building. The hut is scarcely visible from the track above. While it lies below the line of the forest proper, the building is cupped by its own screen of mature trees.

From this approach, it is difficult to perceive fully the hut's location in the valley. The building is more clearly visible to walkers from two of the valley's other tracks. A path from the youth hostel skirts below the tree line, offering oblique glimpses (fig. 8). However, the hut can be seen most distinctly from a track that climbs from the village to follow the opposite slope of the valley at a similar elevation (fig. 9). From this vantage point, one can see three huts of a roughly similar age, quite close together, between the youth hostel and the point of the valley's V. Heidegger's is the highest, a little more distant from its neighbors, at the apex of a convex bank facing almost due south. To the west is a prospect toward the distant Alps, to the east a closer prospect toward the apex of the valley. Heidegger's hut was perhaps the most remote building in the vicinity when built.

8. The hut viewed from a path
between Todtnauberg Youth
Hostel and the hamlet of
Büreten.

9. The hut viewed from across
the valley.

Despite the expansion of the village along the valley floor below, its views retain some sense of its original isolation.

The hut sits on a leveled shelf of ground that both cuts into the valley slope and projects from it (fig. 10). The building surveys the landscape, sheltered and framed by trees (fig. 11). An inclined rubble plinth levels the floor with respect to the shelf. The elevation of the hut that faces the valley has a hipped roof. The roof ridge rises to a height above the walls almost equal to the height of the walls themselves (fig. 12). The hut measures approximately six meters by seven. It is made largely of timber, framed and clad with timber shingles. Windows and the principal door are flush to the wall, with surrounding architraves fitted as cover strips. Three planks held by two timber strings make steps up to the door. The hut's external walls are painted gray. Windows, doors, and shutters are painted in bright colors. Their present hues appear to match those in photographs contemporary with Heidegger's occupation. Window transoms, mullions, and casements are a brilliant white. Their frames are canary yellow and architraves a deep blue. Hinged shutters are painted leaf green. The door is also green, with a blue frame.

The hut appears to have been built with occasional occupancy in mind, and is easily secured when unattended. The first task for returning residents is to unlock the front door and open the hut for occupation. Windows are fitted with a shutter or pair of shutters. When closed, these can be fixed in place with a painted iron bar. This bar, secured through the window frames, can only be released from inside. With the shutters thus opened, the hut's interior is illuminated.

10. Model showing the hut sitting on its leveled shelf of ground, which both cuts into the valley slope and projects from it.

11. The hut surveys the landscape from its leveled shelf of ground.

12. The hut is built into the bank, its timber-framed shingle walls sitting on a rubble plinth. The roof is almost the same height again as the walls.

Inside the Hut

The hut has three main rooms, illustrated here by the plan, sections, and model (figs. 13, 14, 15). All rooms are subdivided further into locations specific to particular uses, labeled as follows on the plan. The front door (1), on the face of the hut perpendicular to the valley, opens outward. Just inside is a storm porch (2), with a row of coat hooks on each side. An inner door opens from the porch onto the *Vorraum,* literally the "fore" or "front" room (3). This occupies the western edge of the hut, containing a dining area behind the porch, a heating stove (4), a cooking stove (5), equipment for preparing food, and a bed (6). Behind the door-swing of the porch's inner door is a further door, which opens to the bedroom (7). This room is tightly packed with beds (8) and a small table for washing (9). Beyond is a room that was Heidegger's study (10), where his desk (11) and table (12) remain. Another bed was also kept in the corner here (13). Two further rooms are reached from the north of the *Vorraum.* These are built next to the retaining wall against the hillside: an earth closet (14) and drying room (15). The latter has a door opening directly to the exterior, to the north of the hut's eastern side.

The plan of the hut is divided almost equally in four (fig. 16). The central partition running north-south is aligned with its edge against the building's center line. The *Vorraum* is thus slightly wider than its neighbors. The east-west wall is made as a full-height partition where it separates the bedroom from the study, with a division on the same line implied by a cupboard and an overhead shelf in the *Vorraum.* The hipped roof has a ridge running north-south. The two hips and ridge are approximately equal thirds of the hut's length in plan. The roof is centered over the principal rooms, its northern slope continuing downward over the drying room and earth closet to a roughly built gutter along the top of the retaining wall against the bank.

The hut is primarily a timber-framed structure. Details of its construction suggest that it was made and assembled using hand tools. Walls are framed using a series of vertical studs, braced with horizontal members and filled with rubble. Some pockets in this frame are fitted with window frames. Externally, walls are clad with timber shingles in equal courses, lapped in two directions (fig. 17). Internally, walls are lined with vertical

13. Plan of the hut.

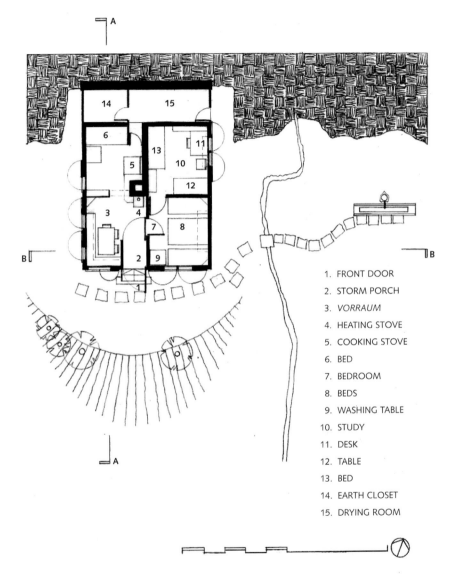

1. FRONT DOOR
2. STORM PORCH
3. *VORRAUM*
4. HEATING STOVE
5. COOKING STOVE
6. BED
7. BEDROOM
8. BEDS
9. WASHING TABLE
10. STUDY
11. DESK
12. TABLE
13. BED
14. EARTH CLOSET
15. DRYING ROOM

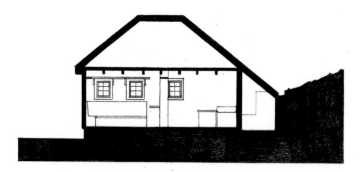

14. Sections of the hut.

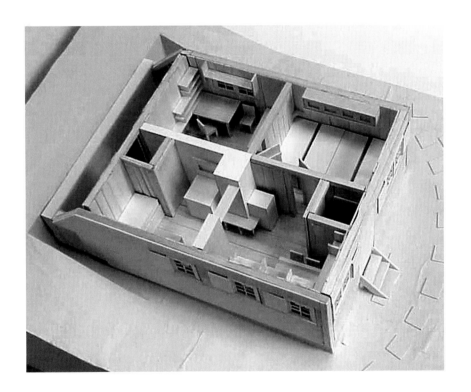

15. Model of the hut.

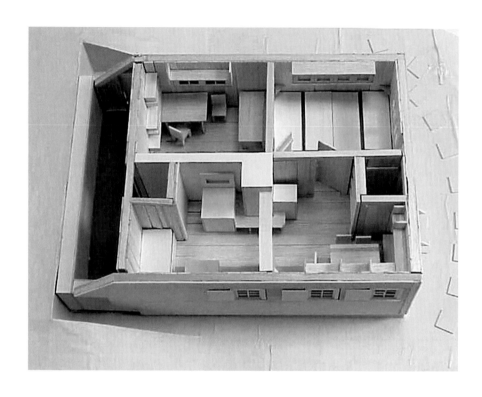

16. The plan of the hut is
divided almost equally in four.
The *Vorraum* runs across the
bottom of the model here.

17. Externally, walls are clad
with timber shingles in equal
courses, lapped in two
directions.

planks, finished and treated, of approximately equal size and spacing. The exception to this is the east wall of the drying room, where the frame of the hut is finished only on the outside and left exposed within. The north-south dividing wall is made of masonry at its northern end, providing a structurally stable core to the building. This wall also incorporates the chimney stack, which collects fumes from flues to both stoves noted above. The wall is finished with a rough render that has been painted. Where the chimney emerges from the roof ridge, it is in clay brick. The floor is made from timber planks laid north-south. These are presumably fixed to joists that span between the building's masonry plinth and the masonry spine wall. The roof structure appears to spring from a wall plate fixed to the outside face of wall frames. From the arrangement of shingles, it seems that the roof is made with purlins fixed to rafters which carry horizontal battens. Covering shingles, thinner and larger than those on the walls, are nailed in place. On the southernmost roof slope is one inset glass tile, which lights the roofspace.

Rooms of the hut contain some fixed furniture, much of which dates from the time of construction. Movable furniture appears to be arranged largely as it has been since the hut was built. Like most of the building, the furniture is made from timber.

The southernmost half of the *Vorraum* was arranged as a dining room (figs. 18, 19, 20). The porch occupies a corner of the room. Tucked against this, turning a corner around the external wall, is fixed a wooden bench. It is padded with cushions, and some photographs show a piece of fabric stretched against it as a seatback. A table stands at the return of the bench. In addition to the bench, there are three chairs around the table. Above the bench are three windows, a double-leaf side-hung casement facing south and two single-leaf side-hung casements facing west. Directly over the architrave is a continuous timber shelf supported on brackets cut from planks and fixed to the walls between windows. In the very corner of the room photographs show a hook for bags. As with all rooms in the hut, ceiling beams are exposed. Between them, approximately centered between the walls, hangs a single lamp—originally oil, but substituted with an electric bulb in later years of the philosopher's occupation.[22] Against the return wall of the storm porch, above the table, was hung a portrait of the poet and writer Johann Friedrich Hebel.[23]

19. Heidegger, at the corner of
the dining table, in
conversation. (Copyright Digne
Meller-Marcovicz.)

20. Heidegger sitting at the
head of the dining table, laid for
a meal, with condensation
trickling down the windows.
(Copyright Digne Meller-
Marcovicz.)

The *Vorraum* is divided in two by an overhead shelf and a cupboard, to which a decorated clock was fixed. In the southern half of the *Vorraum*, opposite the dining table, is an iron heating stove (fig. 21). A flue rises from the top of this stove, offsetting at a high level into the adjacent chimney breast. Another wooden bench is fixed against the stove, with a shelf beneath, running along the chimney into the northern half of the *Vorraum*, which serves as the hut's kitchen. Here is another stove, containing an oven and six hotplates (fig. 22). Behind this cooking stove is a tiled splashback with integral tiled shelves. In photographs, there is a woven carpet directly in front of the cooking stove, approximately one meter by two. On the external wall opposite the cooking stove is a single-leaf side-hung casement window. Beneath this is a leather-topped wooden chest. At the north end of the room, between the external wall and the return of the door to the drying room, is a bed.

In the main bedroom, much of the floor area is occupied by four beds (figs. 23, 24). Mattresses are set on a base with timber sides; their tops are just below the windowsill. This window, a double-leaf side-hung casement, faces south. Between the window and the hut's central partition is a table. Above the beds are two cabinets, each with double doors. In the two eastern corners of the room are triangular shelves, probably made for candles. When the hut was equipped with electric light, a bulb was fitted above the washing table. A picture of a woman in *Schwarzwald* costume and a warming pan appear to be hung on the north wall in photographs.

Heidegger's study is reached through a door in this wall of the bedroom (figs. 25, 26, 27). Diagonally opposite the door is a desk measuring approximately one by one-and-a-half meters. Above it is a window, identical in dimension to that in the bedroom, but facing east. To the other side of the window is another table, smaller than the desk. Set into the corner of the room, running along the northern wall, is a series of shelves. Behind the desk, beyond the door-swing, is another bed. Two electric table lamps were later provided: one on the desk, another on the shelves. Outside the window of the study was hung a chime, a "windwheel."

The configuration of the hut's interior appears to have followed particular activities that occurred there. A direct relationship is apparent between purpose and arrangement.

21. The kitchen area of the *Vorraum*. The heating stove is to the right of the philosopher. Elfride Heidegger is preparing food on top of the low chest next to the bed. (Copyright Digne Meller-Marcovicz.)

22. The cooking stove in the
kitchen and adjacent low
bench. Elfride Heidegger cooks
while her husband looks on.
(Copyright Digne Meller-
Marcovicz.)

23. The bedroom, with Heidegger emerging from his study. Towels are hung on the back of the door to the *Vorraum*. A warming pan and picture of a woman in traditional Black Forest clothing are fixed to the wall. (Copyright Digne Meller-Marcovicz.)

24. The bedroom, with the washing table to the right. Flannels hang from a small mirror-fronted cabinet. A toy boat is setting sail on the ocean of the mattress. (Copyright Digne Meller-Marcovicz.)

25. The study from the bedroom door. Shelves are seen almost empty apart from a few manuscripts. The philosopher's pens, writing mat, and blotter are arranged on the desk. (Copyright Digne Meller-Marcovicz.)

26. Heidegger poses at his desk
looking toward the top of the
valley, his manuscripts on the
shelves behind. (Copyright
Digne Meller-Marcovicz.)

27. Another posed view of
Heidegger at his desk. The bed
in the study is visible behind the
philosopher's chair. (Copyright
Digne Meller-Marcovicz.)

Decoration was spare, with little elaboration beyond the coloring of window frames, the working of some loose furniture, and the profiling of shelf brackets. Much of the building's layout and detail involved the straightforward application of chosen construction methods.

Outside the Hut

Immediately south of the hut is a leveled mound, roughly centered on the building's front door. It is likely that this mound was made specifically for the hut with material taken from a corresponding cut behind. A number of trees grow from the bank in front of the dining area windows (fig. 28). A simple bench may be seen beneath the bedroom window in photographs from 1968, but has since been removed. The upper surface of this bench was a single plank, fixed to two stanchions made from cut sections of log. The photograph shows a towel left hanging to dry from this bench, which was presumably used for airing in warmer months (fig. 29).

A few paces outside the drying room's external door is a shallow stream running down the valley slope. Beyond this is a well (figs. 30, 31). A split, hollowed log is fed with water from a spout in another, upright log connected to a natural spring. A star carved in relief from a timber cube sits on this upright. A number of stone slabs make a path connecting the well with the leveled shelf in front of the hut and the main door.

28. The hut in 1968 with Heidegger and his wife sitting in deckchairs on the leveled mound outside, looking toward the village and distant view to the Alps. The valley appears far less built up than it is now. (Copyright Digne Meller-Marcovicz.)

29. The front of the hut,
showing the entrance steps and
storm porch with coats hung
from both sides. (Copyright
Digne Meller-Marcovicz.)

31. Heidegger walking back to
the hut, having filled a bucket
with water at the well.
(Copyright Digne Meller-
Marcovicz.)

32. Karl Löwith's photograph
of the hut in winter 1922,
shortly after construction.
(From Karl Löwith, *Mein Leben
in Deutschland vor
und nach 1933.* Copyright
1986 J. B. Metzler'sche
Verlagsbuchhandlung and
C. E. Poeschel Verlag GmbH,
Stuttgart.)

HOW THE HUT CAME TO BE BUILT

Details of circumstances surrounding the construction of the hut in the summer of 1922 remain unclear (fig. 32). However, some information exists concerning Heidegger's motivations for building the hut, the choice of site, and his own role in the construction process.

Starting in January 1922, Heidegger became involved in negotiations toward what was to be his first appointment to a chair of philosophy, at Marburg University.[24] This prospective change in circumstances appears to have offered four related reasons to build the hut. First, the post would offer Heidegger, then thirty-three, his first significant source of independent income. Second, the appointment would require him to move away from familiar territory.[25] About four hundred kilometers to the north, Marburg is distant from the area Heidegger knew well, having been born and raised in a town on the edge of the Black Forest, attended boarding school at nearby Konstanz, and pursued undergraduate and postgraduate study at university in Freiburg. Heidegger and his young family appear to have wanted to maintain a base in southern Germany while he was teaching elsewhere. Third, the philosopher needed a place to keep up his research, to think and write.[26] Fourth, there is some evidence to suggest that Heidegger perceived a romantic allure in building a retreat.[27] The combination of these circumstances appears to have been decisive. An attempt was made to arrange a retreat in the Black Forest where he might be able to work. A suitable site was found, and work on the hut began.

Heidegger appears to have sought particular conditions of the Black Forest region that would help him to sustain his intellectual activity. His motivation appears to have derived partly from his upbringing. He had become interested in theological and philosophical questions during a childhood circumscribed by rhythms of the countryside and his role in the local church.[28] Although his thought later led him away from institutionalized Catholicism, he maintained working patterns similar to those established in his youth. He remained fond of locations like those in which he had begun to think philosophically. They appear to have been something of a datum for him in his early explorations of thought. By contrast, Heidegger claimed to have found the university milieu unconducive to work. On returning to Marburg from the hut, he wrote to Karl Jaspers describing his academic environment as "the stuffy, stifling atmosphere that envelops one again. . . . I have no desire to spend my time with University professors."[29] His preference for the country continued throughout his life. It preserved for him "the enigma of what abides and what is great."[30] Information suggests that his motivations in building the hut derived from both an empathy with familiar situations and a preference for possibilities offered by the rural.

Although Heidegger was clearly sensitive to an appreciation of provincial surroundings, circumstances that led him specifically to Todtnauberg in search of a building site are not clear. Heinrich Wiegand Petzet and Walter Biemel intimate that the immediate landscape was important. It is likely that Heidegger was already familiar with the district; indeed, there is a published photograph of Heidegger and Edmund Husserl dated 1921, a year before construction of the hut, which appears to have been taken above Todtnauberg (fig. 33).[31] The paths described above from which the hut may be seen lead beyond the V-shaped valley to the Stübenwasen ridge, which is traversed by long-distance regional paths. Heidegger would have known of these as a keen walker and cross-country skier,[32] and it appears that Elfride Heidegger was also already familiar with the area.[33] If Heidegger and his family were seeking a site for a hut in familiar territory, this site certainly includes aspects of landscape characteristic of the Black Forest region. Also, more practically for a commuting academic, the locality has the only railway in the Black Forest highlands. It is served by a station named Feldberg (close to a village of that name some distance to the east of the peak) on a route climbing from Freiburg to Titisee and Schluchsee.

As suggested above, Heidegger's attraction to the landscape around Todtnauberg was connected with his philosophical work (fig. 34). While he considered familiar rural

33. A photograph from
the collection of Karl
Löwith dated 1921 showing
Heidegger with Edmund
Husserl. It appears that
this picture was taken
above Todtnauberg. (From
Karl Löwith, *Mein Leben
in Deutschland vor
und nach 1933*. Copyright
1986 J. B. Metzler'sche
Verlagsbuchhandlung and
C. E. Poeschel Verlag GmbH,
Stuttgart.)

34. The valley containing the
village of Todtnauberg, looking
south toward the Alps.

surroundings to be a prompt for thinking, it was particularly in cycles of nature that he claimed sustenance for intellectual exploration. For Heidegger, movements of nature were resonant and essential, close to existence and to what he came to term "things." Although Heidegger was to write about this topic later in life, it seems probable that he already had an intuition for such sentiments in 1922.[34] In building the hut, Heidegger and his family likely sought proximity to the forces of nature—which Todtnauberg and its climate offered at high concentration.

Events surrounding construction of the hut remain unclear. Little information has been found. Gertrud Heidegger reports that the plot chosen at Todtnauberg was acquired cheaply. The local farmer sold it readily because of waterlogging from the adjacent stream. Building work was executed during summer 1922. Elfride Heidegger, the philosopher's wife, "organized and supervised" construction.[35] It has been suggested that builders were local men from the Todtnauberg hamlet of Büreten, below the site, led by farmer and joiner Pius Schweizer.[36] The authorship of the design is unclear, however, and it is not known whether an architect was involved. It has also been impossible to establish precisely what was Heidegger's role, if any, in initial building work at the hut. Although the philosopher's involvement in construction was not direct, it is likely that he would have taken an interest in the layout and progress of the building.

HOW THE HUT WAS USED

The hut was intended as somewhere for Heidegger to work. Throughout his career, he retreated there when commitments allowed and when he felt in need of concentration. Many of his most famous philosophical writings were prepared there. After the hut's construction, Heidegger visited Todtnauberg frequently, with some extended periods of residence. Only old age and frailty eventually limited his visits.

The hut was never Heidegger's sole residence. He always maintained a base in the town of his academy; he rented rooms in Marburg until 1928 and then lived in a newly built house in Freiburg (discussed below). When teaching in Marburg, Heidegger's visits to Todtnauberg were limited mostly to breaks between semesters of teaching. After he became professor in Freiburg in 1928, he was close enough to the hut to visit also for extended weekends. Heidegger sometimes walked the eighteen kilometers to the hut from Freiburg, including eight hundred meters of climb, setting out early in the morning.[37]

Heidegger used the hut as a base for walks and ski tours of the surrounding landscape (fig. 35). Explorations of the immediate terrain became a sustaining part of his residence at Todtnauberg. In younger years, Heidegger was also a participant in seasonal occupations of valley life, assisting villagers with autumn forestry, felling trees, and preparing logs for seasoning.[38]

Heidegger often used the hut alone, although he shared it with both occasional visitors and family—he and Elfride Heidegger had two young sons when the hut was built. Heidegger seems to have considered Todtnauberg partly as somewhere to escape from family life. He guarded work time even when others were present. While finalizing *Being and Time* during 1926 and 1927, he rented a room in a house nearby to enable him

35. Heidegger on a path in the trees above the hut. (Copyright Digne Meller-Marcovicz.)

to study when his young family stayed at the hut.[39] Gertrud Heidegger reports how, in later years, her grandmother continued to keep the children quiet while her grandfather worked. Generally, visitors were permitted only alone or in small numbers, when work allowed, and usually when Elfride Heidegger was there.

Later in life, Heidegger allowed fewer visitors. Most were occasional day guests. However, in the 1920s and early 1930s, Heidegger invited small groups of his closest— mainly graduate—students to summer seminars at the hut. Karl Löwith wrote of the hut "where the more intimate circle of students often spent hospitable weeks."[40] A camp was set up on the hillside and evening discussion carried on around a fire. Rüdiger Safranski writes:

Students of . . . [the philosopher's] circle were allowed to visit Heidegger at his cabin at Todtnauberg. There, the secret king of philosophy held court in the *Bündische Jugend* manner. At the summer solstice, wheels of fire were sent rolling down-hill. Heidegger called out strong words after them. Sometimes he made a speech. "To be by the fire at night . . ." he began on one occasion, and with the next sentence was back with his beloved Greeks. Parmenides in Todtnauberg.[41]

Shortly after Heidegger's appointment to the rectorship of Freiburg University in 1933, he convened a similar event in the valley below the hut, an "academic summer camp" for colleagues and students who were members of the Nazi party to discuss university organization under the new regime.[42] Heidegger discussed this event in the apologia for his rectorship, which Hugo Ott has examined in detail in comparison with contemporary accounts.[43]

The hut's occupants were required to fulfill a number of tasks to maintain their existence once the hut was opened for use—principally, preparing and maintaining the fire, preparing food, eating, sleeping, washing, and writing. The division of tasks between Martin and Elfride Heidegger when at Todtnauberg together is unclear, although it appears that conventional domestic arrangements applied. For example, Elfride Heidegger attends the stove in photographs while her husband sits on the adjacent bench.

Needs of subsistence, especially those for heat and light, influenced experience at the hut. Only later in Heidegger's occupation of the building was it connected to any public utilities. Its internal climate benefits from an opportune arrangement with respect to natural heat and light. The alignment of the hut corresponds almost exactly with the cardinal points of the compass, the front to the south, opening toward midday sun, and the back sheltered against the north. Rooms inside thus receive sunlight at different times of day. The dining table catches lunchtime southern sun and dinnertime western sun. The bedroom faces south, so that morning sun from the east lights the washing table placed on the room's west side. The study window receives sunlight early in the morning, when Heidegger liked to work.[44] This window also affords a distant view toward the top of the valley. In addition to their orientation, the windows are part of the hut's climatic system. They have two layers of glazing, both of which open for variable degrees of ventilation (fig. 36). The outer shutter also assists in this.

Natural heat and light are supplemented with artificial sources. The hut has two proprietary cast-iron wood-burning stoves, one in the *Vorraum* giving warmth, the other in the kitchen area providing heat for cooking. Until electricity was fitted, these stoves were the principal source of heat. They had to be laid, tended, and cleared—the latter all year round. Wood for burning was taken from the surrounding forest. As a resident of the valley, Heidegger was permitted a cord: an allotted number of trees in the surrounding forest that he could cut for firewood. Chopping logs for the fire was an occasional task when the philosopher was in residence at the hut. These were stored in the drying room and stacked under the eaves, where they helped to insulate the interior from winter cold. The masonry wall against which the stoves were fixed also acted as a heat-store, retaining and reemitting heat slower than surrounding timber walls. The wood burnt by the stoves provided some artificial light, supplemented by candles and oil lamps until electric light was introduced.

Sources of heat and light allowed other activities in the hut when Heidegger was resident. Food preparation occurred in the kitchen area of the *Vorraum*. The stove provided an oven and hotplates for cooking. Above it was a tiled splashback with an inset shelf for hot pots. Food preparation was carried out on two surfaces: the top of the

36. The hut's windows have two layers of glazing, both of which open for variable degrees of ventilation. Some windows—like this one to the dining area—also have an additional small opening light in the outer leaf.

high chest placed beneath the window, and a low shelf also used as a bench to the right of the stove. A number of hooks were arranged between the beams of the ceiling. Here cloths were hung, handy for use and kept dry by rising heat from the stove (fig. 37). Washing up was done either in the kitchen, with water carried through in buckets, or directly at the well.

Eating occurred mostly at the dining table in the *Vorraum,* with food brought through from the kitchen (fig. 38). The table was set for both drinks and meals, for different courses and combinations of diners. It appears that Heidegger sat at the head of the table here. When not in use, crockery was stored along a shelf above the table, laid on edge and restrained from falling by a timber rail.

As has already been noted, there are six beds in the hut: one in the kitchen, one in the study, and four packed into the main bedroom. Each of these beds has a timber frame raised above the floor. In photographs, mattresses and pillows appear to have had hair stuffing. Beds were clothed with bedspread, sheets, and blankets according to the season. Gertrud Heidegger reports that the kitchen bed was the most popular, since it was warmest due to the proximity of the stove and insulation provided by logs in the drying room behind.

A table for washing was provided in the principal bedroom. There was also an enamel washtub that could be used inside or outside. Above the washing table was a mirror-fronted cabinet for the storage of various requisites. Photographs show brushes and shaving equipment arranged on the tabletop. Beneath the cabinet were hooks holding flannels. More hooks, fixed to the wall immediately adjacent and to the back of the bedroom door, were provided for towels. The earth closet adjacent to the drying room provided for sanitary needs.

Heidegger worked principally in the study: thinking, reading, checking proofs for publication, or writing. The desk remains beneath the window. On its surface was a leather writing mat, an inkwell, a blotter, and a wooden tray for pens. Oil lamps that originally allowed him to work at night were later replaced with electric lights. Manuscripts were written longhand on loose-leaf paper and stored on adjacent shelves.[45] Heidegger kept his library at his city house, and there are few books in photographs of

37. Heidegger lacing his boots in the kitchen. (Copyright Digne Meller-Marcovicz.)

the hut's study. A chair for visitors separated the desk from another table, used for layout. There was also a bed in the room. Hung on the wall was a portrait of Friedrich von Schelling. When weather permitted, Heidegger liked to work at a desk outside.[46] He set up a table on the leveled ground in front of the hut, facing the westerly prospect toward the Alps.

With the hut used partly as a base for forest excursions, provision was made for storage and drying of outdoor clothing. Shoes were kept in the kitchen, beneath the bench adjacent to the stove used as a seat and worktop, which also doubled for lacing boots. Garments were kept in the storm porch, which was lined with hooks. Heidegger enjoyed skiing and skis were stored in the drying room.

For Heidegger, the hut sat in a providential landscape. Some of the waters rising in the vicinity of Todtnauberg flow into the Danube, and he remained deeply aware of the interpretation of that river's course by the poet Friedrich Hölderlin. In the poem "Der Ister"—taking the classical name for the Danube—Hölderlin writes of the river as almost flowing backward. He casts its destination toward the Black Sea as the mythopoetic landscape of ancient Greece, a metaphorical source, and its beginnings in the west as a golden age Hesperia.[47] This landscape, for Hölderlin and for Heidegger, was somewhere that great things could and should take place.

Heidegger wrote about his hut, its surroundings, and his involvement with them on a number of occasions during his life. In each instance, to a varying extent, he interpreted the hut and its landscape with his philosophical vocabulary. There are a number of references to Todtnauberg, for example in his correspondence with Karl Jaspers from the early 1920s. Rüdiger Safranski has translated extracts from this correspondence in his Heidegger biography:

I'm off to the cabin—and am looking forward a lot to the strong mountain air—this soft light stuff down here ruins one in the long run. Eight days lumbering—then again writing. . . . It's late night already—the storm is sweeping over the hill, the beams are creaking in the cabin, life lies pure, simple and great before the soul. . . . Sometimes I no longer understand that down there one can play such strange roles.[48]

In letters from Todtnauberg, Heidegger wrote of life in the city and university as *unten,* literally "under" or "below." Life at the hut was *oben,* "above," superior; he came to refer to it as "up there." The epithet described concentrated writing mixed with walking, skiing, and—in younger days—assisting the locals with forestry. It indicated Heidegger's attribution of a special legitimacy to his relationship with the hut and its enveloping seasonal movements.

In 1934, Heidegger was offered the chair of philosophy in Berlin, arguably the most prestigious appointment in Germany. He turned it down. Life at the hut was central to the polemic of his official justification, first recorded as a radio address and published as a newspaper article, translated as "Why Do I Stay in the Provinces?":

On the steep slope of a wide mountain valley in the southern Black Forest, at an elevation of 1150 metres, there stands a small ski hut. The floor plan measures six metres by seven. The low-hanging roof covers three rooms: the kitchen which is also the living room, a bedroom and a study. . . .

This is my work-world. . . . Strictly speaking I myself never observe the landscape. I experience its hourly changes, day and night, in the great comings and goings of the seasons. The gravity of the mountains and the hardness of their primeval rock, the slow and deliberate growth of the fir-trees, the brilliant, simple splendour of the meadows in bloom, the rush of the mountain brook in the long autumn night, the stern simplicity of the flatlands covered with snow—all of this moves and flows through and penetrates daily existence up there, and not in forced moments of "aesthetic" immersion or artificial empathy, but only when one's existence stands in its work. It is the work alone that opens up space for the reality that is these mountains. The course of the work remains embedded in what happens in this region.

On a deep winter's night when a wild, pounding snowstorm rages around the cabin and veils and covers everything, that is the perfect time for philosophy. Then its questions become simple and essential. Working through each thought can only be tough and rigorous. The struggle to mould something into language is like the resistance of the towering firs against the storm.

And this philosophical work does not take its course like the aloof studies of some eccentric. It belongs right in the midst of the peasants' work. When the young farmboy drags his heavy sled up the slope and guides it, piled high with beech logs, down the dangerous descent to his house, when the herdsman, lost in thought and slow of step, drives his cattle up the slope, when the farmer in his shed gets the countless shingles ready for his roof, my work is of the same sort. It is intimately rooted in and related to the life of the peasants. . . .

At most a city-dweller gets "stimulated" by a so-called "stay in the country." But my whole work is sustained and guided by the world of these mountains and their people. Lately from time to time my work up there is interrupted by long stretches at conferences, lecture trips, committee meetings and my teaching work down here in Freiburg. But as soon as I go back up there . . . I am simply transported into the work's own rhythm, and in a fundamental sense I am not in control of its hidden law. People in the city often wonder whether one gets lonely up in the mountains among the peasants for such long and monotonous periods of time. But it isn't loneliness, it is solitude. . . . Solitude has the peculiar and original power of not isolating us but projecting our whole existence out into the vast nearness of the presence [*Wesen*] of all things.[49]

Heidegger considered the hut to be small and basic. For him, it had resonant simplicity. The hut, as situated in the valley, was his "work-world." It was a refuge of solitary concentration. To him, it was also a refuge against—but simultaneously with—the elements. Here, Heidegger felt himself in immediate contact with natural forces. For him, these forces stood for the power of creation and an impetus toward philosophy that he found inherent. The mountains' tangible presence and seasonal movements prompted explorations of existence. Heidegger felt that Todtnauberg presented a challenge to "aloof" philosophical wordplay (such as definitions of "aesthetics" and "empathy"). He perceived greater authority in the bluntness of existence he found intensified by mountain terrain. For him, the very "nearness" of the mountain situation preceded interpretation. The material he needed to philosophize was already there laid out before him, although its immediacy belied the complex task of attempting to render its charge in words.

There was a moral dimension to Heidegger's interpretation of the hut and its surroundings. He saw the building, intertwined with the landscape, as somehow honest. It was as direct as the "resistance of the towering firs of the storm" and "the peasants' work" of his neighbors. To Heidegger, there was nobility in an intimate connection with the slopes. He felt that his thought and writing drew from the taproot of situation. Although Heidegger divided his own life between city and mountains (a matter of his choice, as opposed to the necessity of "peasant" subsistence), he was emphatic that the landscape was not a picturesque fancy to be admired by the "city-dweller." To him, there was an ethical contrast between the city—absorbed in its own delusions—and a pastoral life which he perceived as more straightforward. The provincial had a special authority and a unique voice. In the mountains, life and shelter were philosophy as craft, a rigorous exploration of human need. In that situation, for Heidegger, philosophy itself became almost a natural force. Thought at Todtnauberg was not strictly his, having its own "hidden law." This law was itself a matter of moral observance, to be engaged with as part of the terrain's inherent rigor.

In this way, the philosopher valorized his encounters with the landscape. The real debate for him was no human conversation at the academy below, no Socratic dialogue. It was to be had in solitary confrontation between his mind, language, and the raw physical authority he perceived in the terrain and its climate. This was an uncompromising morality. Although Heidegger may have found simplicity in his location, he also perceived there a providential toughness. He described his relationship with Todtnauberg through an almost martial vocabulary: resistant, powerful, vast. Here is the philosopher's "curious yearning for hardness and rigour" given shape by the mountains.[50] Heidegger's Todtnauberg was no aesthete's romance: it was an arena for solitary sparring.

Heidegger shaped philosophical argument from his understanding of mountain life in a 1951 paper titled (without commas) "Building Dwelling Thinking."[51] In that paper, he argued that the procedures and vocabulary of contemporary development had intervened between "building" and "dwelling." Heidegger suggested that these words, in proper relation, named activities that had once been—and, for him, should become again—fundamentally inseparable, conjoined in a "thinking" susceptible to immediacies and enormities of daily existence. This proper relationship was epitomized for him by a traditional Black Forest life, which he promoted with the example of an idealized, conjectural farmhouse:

Let us think for a while of a farmhouse in the Black Forest [*einen Schwarzwaldhof*], which was built some two hundred years ago by the dwelling of peasants [*bäuerliches Wohnen*]. Here the self-sufficiency of the power to let earth, sky, divinities and mortals enter *in simple oneness* into things ordered the house. It placed the farm on the wind-sheltered mountain slope, looking south [*gegen Mittag*], among the meadows close to the spring. It gave it the wide overhanging shingle roof whose proper slope bears up under the burden of snow, and that, reaching deep down, shields the chambers against the storms of the long winter nights. It did not forget the altar nook [*Herrgottswinkel*] behind the dining table [*gemeinsamen Tisch*]; it made room in its chamber for the hallowed places of childbed and "tree of the dead" [*Totenbaum*], for that is what they call a coffin there, and in this way it drafted for the different generations under one roof the sense of their journey through time. A craft that, itself sprung from dwelling, still uses its tools and gear as things, built the farmhouse.[52]

The residents of this farmhouse, for Heidegger, drew sustenance from what was around them, like their plants and animals, "dwelling" in close proximity. His paper had already introduced the "fourfold" of "earth" (*Erde*), "sky" (*Himmel*), "divinities" (*Göttliche*), and "mortals" (*Sterbliche*), each term rich in etymology, an idiosyncratic summary of the fundamental preconditions of existence with which he felt each human stands alone. Like the "hidden law" of ambiguous agency that Heidegger perceived in his own mountain life, it is this "fourfold," through "dwelling," whose "simple one-ness" orders the house and organizes its inhabitants. "Building" and "dwelling," daily activities of physical and social micro-organization, interact as philosophical craft. The sacred places of the house, entwined with necessities of mountain life, were of special importance: the altar corner (*Herrgottswinkel*), community table (*gemeinsamer Tisch*), childbed, and coffin place (*Totenbaum*). Here, to Heidegger, the residents' "building" and "dwelling" at once constituted and celebrated their existence. The farmhouse was a clock of sorts, each sacred place demarcated in time through physical presences and absences. The presence of each individual at the table counted out lives in meals, empty chairs in between perceived as potent absences awaiting the regular occupant's return. The childbed celebrated new life while the coffin place remembered the dead and awaited the living. For Heidegger, these timescales of routine, rite, and generation were surveyed by the ecclesiastical calendar, supervised by the icon of the altar corner. The house both "drafted" and became a memorial to its inhabitants' occupation, their "dwelling" over time recorded physically in making. To the philosopher, this farmhouse traced its residents' understanding of situation: their physical situation denoted by the building's particular relationship with weather and seasons, configured with respect to sun, snow, and wind; and also their broader situation, paced out in rites and routines between birth and death.

It is possible to interpret common threads linking the hut and the conjectural *Schwarzwaldhof,* not least siting, orientation, construction, and involvement with climate. Heidegger visited the farmhouses of his neighbors in the village of Todtnauberg and the nearby hamlets of Rütte and Büreten (figs. 39, 40). When he wrote this passage, he probably had a particular farmhouse in mind—a house fifty meters below the hut, on the same south-facing valley slope, belonging to Johann Brender, in which he rented a room as a study while writing *Being and Time.*[53] It is also possible to suggest that Heidegger's writings about this idealized *Schwarzwaldhof* demarcate aspects of his own hut life. "Why Do I Stay in the Provinces?" outlines the philosopher's perception of a triumphal quiddity to his own being, an awe at his presence that allows the landscape to philosophize with and through him. This echoes his description of an entwined "building" and "dwelling" that body forth the presence of individual human minds and physically record traces of their existence. The table at the hut, presided over by the portrait of Hebel rather than a Catholic icon, can be seen as marking the rites of hut life. Similarly, chopping wood, drawing water from the well, routines of walking and writing—it could be argued— measured out Heidegger's own "building" and "dwelling" at Todtnauberg. As the *Schwarzwaldhof* centered the conjectural world of his hypothetical peasants, it is possible to consider the hut as centering Heidegger's "work-world," providing shelter and containment, its equipment enabling and describing his life and work.

This is one interpretation. However, equally important—and of this Heidegger was aware—was what his hut and the Black Forest farm did not have in common. In "Building Dwelling Thinking," the philosopher acknowledged that the *Schwarzwaldhof* belonged with a lost age, although he advocated the reclamation of its order in new ways left unspecified. The residents of his farmhouse knew no world other than their own; theirs was tightly bounded, demarcated by a small locality and its rooted people,

measured out in seasons, agricultural and domestic work, rigid social structures, faith, and family ties. It is possible that this life persisted in the valley's living memory when Heidegger moved to Todtnauberg, but by 1951 it was surely all but gone. By then, a *Schwarzwaldhof* came equipped with electric light, hot water, radio transmission, and the services of the internal combustion engine. It was plugged in by media and a growing tourist industry to other cultures, to a growing secularism, to international politics and global events. Likewise, the hut, not least because of the ambitions of its inhabitant, was indivisible from a human world with boundaries far beyond the Black Forest. The philosopher dreamed of the lost intellectual and temporal rigor he perceived at Todtnauberg and mythologized the virtues he perceived in it. However, if Heidegger found traces of that life there for himself, they were fragments caught at full stretch: moments of daydream between teaching and other commitments, always supported by a professorial salary. Despite his leanings toward the anti-academic, when working at the hut he nevertheless remained a tactician in the expertise games of professional philosophy, a tendency fatefully epitomized by his attempts at political influence. Although Heidegger carefully sought to submit himself to the rhythms and lessons of the landscape, a parallel life full of human concerns was always somewhere in attendance.

Heidegger's attempted submission to the "hidden law" that he claimed for the mountains is expanded by another of his writings, a curious free-falling text—part prose, part poem—written in 1947 whose English title is "The Thinker as Poet." If Heidegger succeeded in demarcating a "work-world" for himself, this text accounts for the detail of its sometime presence. The text is divided into sections, each of which describes a particular thought and is introduced with a sentence that appears to outline circumstances of that thought for Heidegger. These preliminary sentences have been translated as follows:

When the early morning light quietly grows above the mountains . . .

When the little windwheel outside the cabin window sings in the gathering thunderstorm . . .

When through a rent in the rain-clouded sky a ray of the sun suddenly glides over the gloom of the meadows . . .

40. A group of *Schwarzwaldhöfe* at the hamlet of Rütte in 2005. A recent hotel complex dominates the hillside above.

When in early summer lonely narcissi bloom in the meadow and the rock-rose gleams under the maple . . .

When the wind, shifting quickly, grumbles in the rafters of the cabin and the weather threatens to become nasty . . .

When on a summer's day the butterfly settles on the flower and, wings closed, sways with it in the breeze . . .

When the mountain brook in night's stillness tells of its plunging over the boulders . . .

When in the winter nights snowstorms tear at the cabin and one morning the landscape is hushed in its blanket of snow . . .

When the cowbells keep tinkling from the slopes of the mountain valley where the herds wander slowly . . .

When the evening light, slanting in the woods somewhere, bathes the tree trunks in gold . . .

The text concludes with a poem:

Forests spread
Brooks plunge
Rocks persist
Mist diffuses

Meadows wait
Springs well
Winds dwell
Blessing muses[54]

The introductory sentences and concluding poem appear to detail the detached conditions of Heidegger's furthest retreat. If "Why Do I Stay in the Provinces?" describes an intimate relationship between philosopher, work, and movements of the mountain setting, "The Thinker as Poet" shows the most concentrated moments of that

41. The star cut from a timber block fixed to the well.

relationship. Apparently, prompts to philosophy were to be found in the sunrise and sunset, storms and snow, the chimes of the hut's windwheel, sunlight revealed by parting cloud and the detail of flora and fauna. These aspects of his surroundings, part of the "blessing" of their location, had for him a moral candor. Heidegger claimed that they yielded authority for his work. He considered the philosophy of Todtnauberg to be that of forests, brooks, rocks, mist, meadows, and winds. For Heidegger, these were elemental motions—the core of philosophy "up there," a palpable verity that outreached irrelevances he perceived in life "below."

"The Thinker as Poet" suggests the manner of Heidegger's involvement with the hut and its surroundings, showing the particular things and phenomena there in which he found distance from human affairs. The text notes that "Springs well," and Hermann Heidegger has reiterated that his father found significance in the hut's water source.[55] The spring's water provided sustenance for life at the hut—enabling drinking, cooking, and washing—yet its origin remained unseen.[56] To Heidegger, water, giver of life at Todtnauberg, had a mysterious provenance. He felt this to be physical reality and also metaphor: the source of life was itself mysterious. Also important to the philosopher was the star fitted to the well, carved in relief from a cube of timber (fig. 41). It is not known who made this decoration, or how it came to be fixed there, although it seems to date from the early days of the hut. While the star is an emblem with both Christian and Judaic symbolism, Heidegger seems to have considered it a personal motif.[57] It stood for the wandering thinker, a bright trace against a dark sky. This carved star bound his work symbolically to the spring which was central to the view from his desk, to the hut life it sustained and the resonances of its unseen origin.

Heidegger's writing in the Jaspers correspondence—as well as in "Why Do I Stay in the Provinces?" and "The Thinker as Poet"—suggests another way in which he found the hut significant. He referred to storms "shifting quickly . . . grumbling . . . in the rafters of the cabin." For the philosopher, storms seem to have been moments of intensity. Their destructive force had potential to inspire, to emphasize the frailty of human existence. The ferocity of weather outside the hut reinforced the relative dryness and security inside, giving significance to the building's sheltering potential (fig. 42). Conversely, more

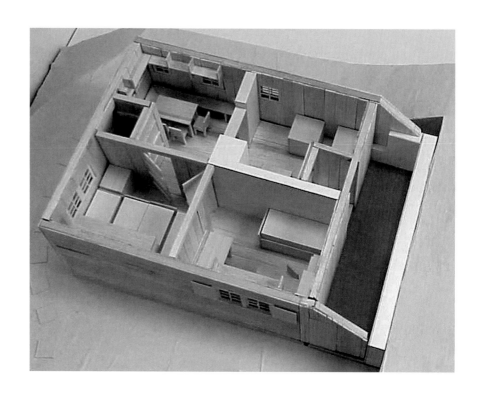

42. The interior of the hut. The
ferocity of weather outside
reinforced the sense of shelter,
the relative dryness and security
inside.

benevolent weather allowed Heidegger to set up a temporary table on flat ground in front of the hut. It is not known whether he kept particular furniture for the purpose or whether furniture was simply brought outside when weather permitted (perhaps furniture in the dining area, which was closest to the door). At this desk, on mild days, the writer sat under the sky and seemingly found direct contact with the inspirational possibilities that he acknowledged in "The Thinker as Poet"—wind, insects, flowers, tracking patches of sun between clouds—giving opportunities for measuring his thought with the surroundings. The wind, in particular, was played by a chime, the "windwheel" noted in "The Thinker as Poet," which hung immediately beyond Heidegger's study window. Its significance to the philosopher is indicated by his request that it be buried with him, along with branches from the forest. Sound from this wheel varied with the wind, reporting its changes. Like the hut's spring, to Heidegger the changing weather was also of mysterious provenance. It too was of practical importance and mystical resonance. The climate conditioned his circumstances as part of the ongoing movement of surroundings that framed his philosophical work.

"The Thinker as Poet" is also a text significant with regard to its historical context. It is important that Heidegger wrote about mountain life in this way in 1947, at such remove from human concerns, distant from a Germany and a Europe then struggling for reconciliation with death and destruction on a vast scale. It was also significant for the philosopher himself, involved in Freiburg University's de-Nazification hearings, struggling to maintain his own livelihood and status. His ability to suspend himself in relation to the surroundings of his hut during this period seems remarkable. His sustained abdication of agency and valorization of mountain existence are striking. Some may perceive evidence here of the durability of Heidegger's philosophy; others will find on his part an astonishing distance from guilt and a facility for detaching himself from human affairs.

It seems that Heidegger enjoyed comparisons between his hut and those of other thinkers. Concluding a chapter of his book *Encounters and Dialogues with Martin Heidegger,* Heinrich Wiegand Petzet wrote:

Kommerell once showed Heidegger in a characteristic posture when he described how . . . in the austere solitude of Todtnauberg's heights, Heidegger sat at a small table in front of the little wooden hut early in the morning and wrote. Heidegger . . . appears in Kommerell's account like one of those sages painted on one of the Chinese folding screens in the Museum of Ethnology in Bremen, *which had inspired Heidegger's great admiration* [my italics]. Each of the sages is sitting in front of his hut, meditating and writing, while a cup—filled by a serving spirit with a refreshing draft from the river that flows by—is passed on to them. Occasionally they engage in discussion, but the river brings them something from the great mystery, without interruption or omission.[58]

Petzet did not date Heidegger's museum visit, but his first visit to Bremen followed construction of the hut.[59] The extent to which Heidegger considered alignments between his hut and other similar buildings is not known. Many bourgeois Germans then and now have kept country retreats of some kind. However, a canonical "tradition" of huts as situations for poetic or philosophical reflection can also be traced back over three thousand years to the Far East.[60] In later life, Heidegger was aware of the work of seventeenth-century Japanese haiku poet Matsuo Basho who worked in a hut like the ones Petzet described.[61] In European culture, one might consider varied "huts" of which he was aware, such as the Tübingen tower of Hölderlin, Goethe's picturesque *Gartenhaus* in Weimar, and Nietzsche's mountain convalescent home at Sils Maria in the Austrian Alps. Important in American literature is Henry David Thoreau's cabin at Walden Pond;[62] other prominent retreats include those of philosopher Ludwig Wittgenstein, Heidegger's approximate contemporary, who had a cabin built at Skjølden in Norway, and of Carl Gustav Jung on the shores of Lake Zurich.[63] Perhaps most significantly, Heidegger was always drawn by the lives of the pre-Socratic philosophers. For the pre-Socratics, for Basho and the Eastern tradition, also arguably for Hölderlin and Nietzsche, philosophy was no arcane bookish pursuit but a life lived through inquiry. In this spirit, many of Heidegger's students and interpreters famed Todtnauberg as the ascetic retreat of a mountain recluse.[64] The philosopher indulged his contemporaries in this view of his hut as the distant retreat of a great mystic, despite, as "Building Dwelling Thinking" implies, his awareness of its limitations. He seems to have enjoyed alignment with this particular canon of thinkers and their huts, endorsing a public image of his mountain life as a heroic confrontation with existence.

Heidegger's letters and writings suggest that, in moments of deepest retreat, he found the involvement of thought and location at Todtnauberg sustaining, providential, and authoritative. As noted above, he sought to distance himself from the city and engage with work at the hut as often as he could, preferring quiet and allowing few visitors. He seems to have enjoyed the belief that his work was a kind of acknowledgment: language taking place through him, in association with the landscape and the hut's mediation of it, demarcated by changefulness experienced in the constancy of solitude. Indeed, the hut and its circumstances seem to have held the possibility of almost hypnotic presence for Heidegger, their particular immediate legitimacy rendering other concerns mundane and, it seems, offering him exemption from implications of life "below."

The philosopher's own interpretations of the hut are expanded by published accounts of visitors. These were few, particularly in later years. When his academic standing grew, the hut became a well-known part of the Heidegger mythology. From the date of his appointment to a chair at the Albert-Ludwig University of Freiburg in 1928, the amount of Heidegger's teaching was reduced and his time turned to research, a change that effectively became absolute with his ban from university teaching between 1945 and 1951. He increasingly retreated to the hut alone, with few visitors permitted: mostly trusted acquaintances.

A visitors' book contains the inscriptions of many prominent contemporary figures from Germany and beyond. Besides Heidegger's family, it appears that the majority of visitors early in the philosopher's career were from his closest circle of students, a number of whom later achieved academic reputations of their own, including Hans-Georg Gadamer and Karl Löwith. Other visitors at this time included Heidegger's teachers and colleagues, such as Edmund Husserl and Karl Jaspers. Later visitors included Jean Beaufret, Herbert Marcuse, Medard Boss, Beda Alleman, Ernst Tugendhat, Karl Friedrich von Weizsäcker, and Paul Celan.[65] Although Heidegger's affair with Hannah Arendt, his student, later a philosopher and political scientist, has been well documented, it is unclear whether she ever visited Todtnauberg.

A regular visitor to the hut in later years was Heinrich Wiegand Petzet, a Heidegger student in Freiburg, subsequently art historian, literary critic, and the philosopher's confidant. Petzet's book, translated as *Encounters and Dialogues with Martin Heidegger,* is effectively Heidegger's authorized biography. The historian made annual autumn visits to Todtnauberg in the 1950s and 1960s, staying at one of the larger *Hütten* near the peak of the Feldberg:

If I wanted to count how many times I took the road from the Stübenwasen to the hut in the fifties and sixties I could only guess, because I was so frequently invited to tea in the afternoon. . . . I could make it in forty minutes, with frequent stops in order to pick the last bluebell, daisy and clover for Frau Heidegger as a decoration for her table. As time passed, I noticed many signposts on this path and was always glad to arrive at the spot where that very old pine tree stood and below which the roof of the hut became visible.

Tea hours were not to take too long; autumn days were becoming too short and Heidegger was anxious to get going. For these walks—"his" walks—which often lasted far into the twilight, were from Heidegger's point of view obviously the real reason for my visiting the hut. The walks we took together often went far—across the mountain at the edge of the forest, toward the summit of the Stübenwasen or toward the Feldbergsträssle. Another path led us toward the west, past the youth hostel and around the "horn," along a wooded slope of the mountain that emerged ahead of us. The latter path offered the possibility of walking side by side and was more appropriate for conversing. . . . On these walks we spoke not only of artists and art works that interested me—professionally or personally—but frequently often of the poetic forces of our time . . . Rilke . . . Gottfried Benn . . . Joseph Conrad. . . .

The walks in the course of which we spoke about artists, poets and often also philosophers always came to an end much too early. Fading light was a warning to return home, and I had still a further way to go. As soon as we arrived at the "entrance gate" where the pathway above the hut branched out, Heidegger would say, "now do take the longer way, not the one through the forest, so that you find your way back home. . . ."[66]

Petzet's account focuses on his impressions of Heidegger, drawing particular attention to personal details of their acquaintance, in which his pride is evident. He saw Todtnauberg as Heidegger's remote province, somewhere that made him almost proof against the outside world. Petzet's Todtnauberg was an experience in which the hut, the landscape, Heidegger, and their conversation were interwoven.

The writer Max Kommerell twice visited Todtnauberg in late summer 1941, first with Hans-Georg Gadamer and subsequently alone. He recorded these visits in a letter to Erika Kommerell, his wife, which was later published in a volume of his correspondence:

We climb up the large and gently winding meadows, passing by the edge of the forest . . . until a shack with a shining roof rises up from the ground. . . . In front of the kitchen, there is a room with a table, a couple of chairs and a very small window.[67] Heidegger emerges from a second room and greets me with a prolonged and peculiar smile. He invites us to sit, pours us a glass of healthy but sour wine from a bottle of Markgräfler. . . . I am free to fathom the face, which is taut and brown and not at all peasantlike, as is often described. It is small, elegant and astute, a little sad, with a certain lostness in the eyes; it is a lostness peculiar to one who, after the most rigorous tests of reason's doubting, reaches the other side of doubt and lives by certainties that he shares with no-one.

Through the small window the sun shines into the dark. . . . Sometimes he [Heidegger] has a delicate smile that is just a tiny, tiny bit crazy. How much I liked him because of that. . . . I thought, "You, with your . . . nods, hints and ways of whisking around until the wife appears and forces you back into your usual motions—you have your own way of living, to which not only the hut but also the landscape belongs, a landscape in which you know every tree and every farmer knows you. In the midst of a famous, active and very public life, you have acquired a measure of solitude, which is necessary for you. Half of the year you surrender yourself here entirely to yourself, and in your work you have the inner passion of consuming yourself. . . . Regardless of whether I grasp your thinking or your thinking grasps me, I greet you as one who takes things seriously and who . . . is pleased to look me in the face and show me the native landscape. . . ."

Another day, he invited me to come alone for a while. . . . It was the most perfect and most immaculate Sunday . . . with the austere solitude of these summits and forest gorges around Feldberg and the long, deeply cut and clearly visible valleys that lie there like the history of a life, especially when the entire chain of the Alps is radiant. . . . Early in the morning, I found him sitting behind a small desk in front of the hut and writing, presumably continuing one of those manuscripts which inside the hut are placed in neat compartments above the writing desk, none of them yet published. . . . He finds his personal dimensions uninteresting and uses himself as a vehicle for problems. Up here his life is a perfect monologue, whereas his reading, as well as his going down to the university and teaching, are increasingly something transitory.[68]

Kommerell saw the Heidegger of Todtnauberg as a solitary writer, happiest in single-minded concentration at some remove from his family and the strictures of academic life. His portrait places philosopher and meaning in harmony. Written while war was raging around Europe, this text chimes with Heidegger's own account in "Why Do I Stay in the Provinces?" Broadly, Kommerell presents a view of Heidegger's hut life that was promoted by his supporters both during his lifetime and after, aligning Heidegger with the philosophy that emerged from the provinces of the pre-Socratics, as well as with Nietzsche's Zarathustra who cursed the city and sought heroic loneliness in the mountains. Some commentary concerning the hut and its owner is less sympathetic, related to Heidegger's involvement with fascism. This connection arguably lies at the heart of the following—most famous—account of the hut, that of the poet Paul Celan.

Celan was a Jew and a survivor of a Nazi forced-labor camp. As a poet writing in German, he thought highly of Heidegger's philosophy. Heidegger also admired Celan's poetry and wanted to meet him. He is reported to have said of Celan's work in 1967: "I know everything of his."[69] When Celan visited Freiburg to give a poetry reading on 24 July 1967, Heidegger invited him to travel to the hut with him the following day. John Felsteiner's biography of Celan contains an account of the visit:

"Heidegger told me," says Hans-Georg Gadamer, "that in the Black Forest, Celan was better informed on plants and animals than he himself was." They also talked about contemporary French philosophy, but Celan's attention was elsewhere. . . . The jewish *Dichter* [poet] accompanied the German *Denker* [thinker] to his mountain retreat at Todtnauberg, noticed midsummer blossoming along the way, took a drink from Heidegger's much publicized well with its star-shaped wooden cube on top, and signed the guest book "with a hope for a coming word in the heart." Later, because the high moorland was too wet, they broke off their walk.[70]

Celan subsequently wrote a poem titled "Todtnauberg" in direct reference to the encounter. Shortly after it was written, he asked his Swiss publisher to make a limited-edition print of this poem, a copy of which he sent to Heidegger. The version later published, with one alteration, has been translated as follows (the alteration is annotated):

Todtnauberg

Arnica, eyebright the
draft from the well with the
star-crowned die [*Sternwürfel*] above it,

in the
hut,

the line
—whose name did the book
register before mine?—,
the line inscribed
in that book about
a hope, today,
of a thinking man's [*eines Denkenden*]
coming[71]
word
in the heart,

woodland sward, unlevelled,
orchid and orchid, single,

coarse stuff, later, clear
in passing,

he who drives us, the man,
who listens in

the half-

trodden fascine [*Knüppel*]

walks over the high moors,

dampness,

much.[72]

The poem has been interpreted by a number of critics, found to be loaded with the charge of a meeting between two men who were intellectual fellow-travelers in many ways, both intent on mining the depths of the German language, but always also Romanian Jew and German. John Felsteiner's interpretation is representative:

[Celan] names the natural world, and these particular flowers signify healing—arnica for bruises, eyebright a balm he remembered from childhood . . . the poet comes as a pilgrim and drinks in conciliation, Heidegger's well . . . signals the yellow badge [that Nazi Germany forced Jews to wear]. . . . The inscription his poem records adds only a little to what Celan actually put in Heidegger's guest book, but—as we're warned by the abrupt "whose name did it take in/ before mine?" which looks back to the 1930s—that little means a lot. The hope in "Todtnauberg" holds "today," "every today" . . . [it] is the hope for the word of "a thinker" who has seemed unable to rethink the unconscionable past. . . . The word "coming" . . . "is the time of the fled gods *and* of the coming God.". . . Again his poem challenges Heidegger noting the "half-/trod . . . paths" of their aborted walk. Yet in an explosive wordplay, Celan's term for "log" (*Knüppel*) also means "bludgeon."[73]

Through the poem "Todtnauberg" Celan engaged with Heidegger and his mountain life in multiple meanings.[74] Celan appears to have found Heidegger physically and intellectually rooted in the landscape. The poet's eye for natural detail and sensitivity to its resonance matched that of the philosopher, but his focus was different.

Celan's appreciation of Heidegger's mountain life was seemingly mediated by his imaginings of what had happened there before. He could not join the philosopher in this most intimate landscape without speculating who might have traveled there in different times and what had been discussed, without intense feeling for the role of the past in this meeting. To Otto Pöggler, the hut itself—like the walk shared by poet and philosopher—reflected barriers between the two men at least as much as it mediated between them:

Is the poet permitted to enter this hut? In his publications, the philosopher made the hut into a sign of identity with the homeland, a rootedness in the land that maintains itself even in the present world civilisation. Whenever Celan himself speaks of a hut, it is of a hut that belongs to another world. . . . The poem "Hüttenfenster" [Hut Windows] in the same volume speaks of those who were scorned, persecuted and exterminated, of the East European Jewry out of which Celan emerged.[75]

Heidegger had gone from a sabbatical semester writing at the hut to take up his rectorship in 1933. After the war, it was to the hut that he turned for refuge and convalescence; he had involved Todtnauberg with Nazism by holding the "academic summer camp" there in October 1933. Celan was aware of these associations and found little meaningful acknowledgment of them from person or place. To Pöggler, it was not just the hut and landscape of Heidegger the susceptible scribe to which Celan was near but could not reach; it was also the transcribed philosophy of that distinctively German province itself.[76] Celan perceived how deeply connected were Todtnauberg and the philosophy that Heidegger claimed from there. To him, the philosophical authority that Heidegger drew from his mountain landscape was as specifically German as it was universal. This notion has been decisive to responses made to Heidegger's hut life by a number of critics, not least Elfride Jelinek, the title of whose drama *Totenauberg* is a wordplay on the location of the hut.[77]

Celan, Petzet, and Kommerell found in their visits to the hut a deep-rooted relationship between Heidegger, his setting, and his work. There seems to be consensus among these observers of the philosopher that his existence at Todtnauberg stood for a life distinctively absorbed with its surroundings. For them, the hut and its landscape described a particular provincialism, one that engaged place and routine, mind and body, thinking and writing, but one associated as much with details of biography as philosophy.

Heidegger's relationship with his surroundings at Todtnauberg—as projected by himself and his visitors—appears to have been rather different from the relationship he had with his city residence. The disparities help to illuminate his relationship with the hut.

As noted above, Heidegger always maintained a residence in the city of his academy, traveling to the mountains when time permitted. From 1923 until 1928, that residence was a set of rented rooms in Marburg. From 1928 until 1971, the philosopher lived in a house built for himself and his family at Zähringen on the edge of Freiburg-im-Breisgau. Thereafter, he spent the five years until his death in a small retirement house built in the garden of the 1928 original.[78] Although little has been traced about the philosopher's residence in Marburg (save his broad dislike of it) or his retirement home, information exists concerning the first Freiburg house and Heidegger's relationship with it (fig. 43). The building still stands and is in the private ownership of his granddaughter Gertrud Heidegger. A short description of the house, Heidegger's life there, and its relationship with the hut is offered here.[79]

Heidegger's appointment to a chair in philosophy at Freiburg from 1928 prompted the building of the house.[80] A building plot was found on the very edge of the city, alongside a country lane earmarked for suburban development named Rötebuckweg. Gertrud Heidegger reports that her grandfather acquired the land for two reasons: because it was comparatively cheap, and because it was close to open country while within a quarter of an hour of the nearest tram. Although the district is now a city suburb, cows grazed there in 1928, with a view of the hilltop ruins of Zähringen Castle behind them. The next step was to appoint an architect, who was named Fetter.[81] Elfride

43. Heidegger's house in
Freiburg-im-Breisgau, from
Rötebuckweg.

Heidegger again directed construction. The philosopher made some input, notably in placing his study and orienting the rooms. The house was built in approximately six months, and the family took up residence in autumn 1928.

The house was built in a similar manner to the hut. It had a stone-filled timber frame, following Black Forest farmhouse tradition (fig. 44). The timber roof carcass was shingle-hung. Walls were clad externally with timber shingles and were plastered or boarded internally. The house has three stories, each with a broadly symmetrical plan (fig. 45). A part-buried basement was used principally for storage. The entrance floor had six principal rooms during Heidegger's occupation: two reception rooms, two sitting rooms, a dining room (fig. 46), and a kitchen. In addition, central to the plan is a large external terrace facing the garden, big enough for a dining table and chairs (fig. 47). The first floor also has six rooms: two children's bedrooms, a master bedroom, a guest bedroom, a bathroom, and Heidegger's study, the largest room in the house (figs. 48, 49, 50). The dining room, upstairs hallway, and master bedroom were organized around Biedermeier furniture inherited from Elfride Heidegger's family, which she was keen to show to good effect. "Biedermeier" describes a period in the German restoration from approximately 1815 to 1848; its furniture celebrated petit bourgeois domesticity: heavy, rustic, and "homely."[82]

Although Heidegger wrote about many locations important to his life—especially the hut—and despite a later fondness for autobiography, he did not write about the Freiburg house in any detail. There is, however, an account by Elfride Heidegger describing the visit of a hypothetical student to the house. This has been quoted in full by Heinrich Wiegand Petzet:

The young man walks across the straight garden path between the flower beds toward the door of the house and climbs a couple of steps under a small roof designed for protection from the rain. However, before he rings the bell, beside which he reads on a little card "Visits after 5 P.M."—he is surprised. For above the wooden beam of the door, a proverb from the Bible is engraved, something he did not expect to find here.[83] Thus unexpectedly attuned to reflectiveness, he is confronted with another surprise on entering the house. The foyer is wide,

4. The front elevation of
Heidegger's city house.

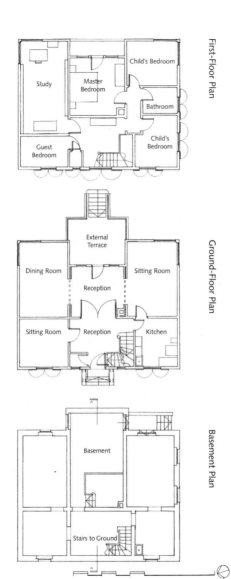

Child's Bedroom

Study

Master Bedroom

Bathroom

Guest Bedroom

Child's Bedroom

External Terrace

Dining Room

Sitting Room

Reception

Sitting Room

Reception

Kitchen

45. Plans of Heidegger's house.

Basement

Stairs to Ground

46. Heidegger in the dining
room of his city house.
(Copyright Digne Meller-
Marcovicz.)

47. Heidegger in the back garden at Rötebuckweg. The external terrace with its dining table and chairs is central to the ground floor of the house, partially covered by the bedroom balcony above. (Copyright Digne Meller-Marcovicz.)

49. Heidegger at his desk.
Manuscripts are arranged in
shelves alongside, the
philosopher's library filling the
room behind. (Copyright Digne
Meller-Marcovicz.)

50. Heidegger in the easy chair alongside his desk. (Copyright Digne Meller-Marcovicz.)

separated by a floor-to-ceiling glass wall, and opens into a single, bright room in which there is a piano and an old armchair. Behind these is another large window, which reaches to the floor and opens onto a terrace half-covered by a protruding higher floor. The terrace provides a place for sitting and in summertime is the center of life for the family. Wide steps lead from the terrace to a garden full of flowers. Thus upon entering the house, the visitor is enveloped by the whole radiating expanse of the meadows and the dark edge of the forest beyond. This is a house that "seems to absorb the whole of nature." Adalbert Stifter[84] would have loved this house.

A door is open on the side towards the dining room with a few beautiful pieces of furniture from the Biedermeier period. The waiting student, however, has no more time to look around, because he must now climb a well turned stairway—a craftsman's masterwork—to the next floor, where beside a huge closet a clock, made in Hellerau, hangs on the wall—the pride of the family. Now things become serious: The professor is waiting.[85]

Elfride Heidegger's description of the house is structured around how the building would influence a stranger's impression. She seems to have been concerned with the house as a suitable expression of her husband's civic and academic role. This expression was given form by an impressive axial view from the front door, a procession to Heidegger's study, and the calculated display of fine furniture. Elfride Heidegger appears to have had particular feelings about the building's status as a professor's house. Given her supervisorial involvement in construction, it seems likely that these compositional devices of its architecture expressed and served her social aspirations.

An account survives by a student visitor similar to the one imagined by Elfride Heidegger. Reiner Schürmann visited Freiburg in 1969. Then a Dominican novitiate, he later became professor of philosophy at the New School in New York. He wrote:

I have just returned from Heidegger's house. It was a real late-afternoon reception about the mystery of being. . . . To begin with the folkloric aspect of the visit, I had my fill and more: a pious inscription above the door . . . ; a small man who looked like a peasant . . . let me in nearly without saying a word into a room that looked rather like a blockhouse; two glasses and a bottle on a small tray; and, especially, a two-hour long conversation which ended up, at least outwardly, in complete darkness. I knew that among things country he had a fondness for . . .

the traditional: his writings speak of the pitcher of cool water, of the peasant's rough hands, of mud-caked clogs and such. I now know that he also likes discussions in the dark. However, the man is so shrewd, and . . . it felt like my meagre schoolboy questions were received by warm and reassuring hands.[86]

Schürmann appears to have interpreted the house as Elfride Heidegger hoped, somewhat in awe of her husband's intellectual stature. However, he also perceived the building through his reading of Heidegger's work, seeing it as part of a personal mythology surrounding the philosopher's thought.

In Freiburg, the Heidegger household was organized according to traditional family roles. The master bedroom, shared marital realm, was central to the plan of the upper floor of the house. The children's realms were somewhat detached from their parents by day but were close to Martin and Elfride's bedroom at night. Heidegger had his own domain in the study (fig. 51). Elfride Heidegger's territory, the kitchen, was less distinctly personal. Family roles were thus determined more emphatically by the Freiburg house than at the hut.

Although farmhouse construction techniques follow tradition in Todtnauberg, they are by no means typical of Freiburg. Nearly one thousand meters below the hut, building traditions in the city are different. Older buildings within the city perimeter were densely packed in long, thin plots with ornamental fronts, made of timber or masonry. The city also had a more recent tradition of suburban building by 1928. Houses of masonry construction employed newer building techniques: tighter construction affording better insulation; reinforced concrete lintels and improved glass-making techniques allowing bigger windows; with mains services provided—electric light, sanitation, and hot and cold running water. Despite its timber frame and shingle cladding, Heidegger's Freiburg house is closer to this more modern tradition. It is effectively a suburban house in Black Forest clothing. Although it shares certain superficial characteristics with *Schwarzwald* houses, it is otherwise built around statutory services with large, extensively glazed rooms. Farmhouse construction methods used in Todtnauberg followed local materials and experience, but such techniques used then in Freiburg stand as affectation.

Affectation is also displayed in the intention to use the house to display Elfride Heidegger's Biedermeier furniture. Martin and Elfride Heidegger were aware that these pieces were loaded with the period's romanticized and aestheticized rustic values. The decision to contrive a setting for this furniture reports an aesthetic sympathy for which there is little evidence at the hut.

The house indicates a suburban tension between aspirations toward a provincial situation and the desire to build a family residence with contemporary comforts close to the city and transportation. Modern comfort appears to have been a driving issue in building the house, whereas there is little indication of such priority in the building of the hut at Todtnauberg. Moreover, the house was conceived with sensitivity to appearances, both social and aesthetic. Heidegger's existence at the Freiburg house—for many years his principal residence when not at Todtnauberg—seems to have been rather different from that he maintained in the mountains. It projected a number of social and intellectual priorities less evident at the hut. Heidegger's lack of writing about the house suggests his ambivalence toward the building and his family life, which is notable in contrast with his stated enthusiasm for solitary existence in the mountains and his perception of philosophical resonance there.

51. Heidegger among the things of his study at Rötebuckweg. (Copyright Digne Meller-Marcovicz.)

THE HUT AS A REFLECTION OF HEIDEGGER'S THINKING?

Heidegger's rhetoric of hut life located him in rigorous contact with existence. He cast the building and its surroundings as participants in active questions of presence. To him, the structure framed its inhabitants and surroundings acutely, tracing flickers of insight. The hut, its equipment, and its small places became empty vessels, allowing the powerful possibility of human occupation. He felt that its basic comforts put him in unusually exacting contact with the weather and the forest's flora and fauna, with whose perceived motions he sought to demarcate existence. Heidegger attributed philosophical authority to the order he found in these things and phenomena. For him, Todtnauberg measured the world in moments of retreat. At deepest remove, he responded to the hut and its mountains through a routine of almost monastic subsistence, affirming there his belief in a liturgy of being and delineating life by its passage in routine.

By contrast with his engagement in this setting, Heidegger apparently felt little resonance with his suburban house and its associated affairs. He seems to have understood Rötebuckweg as a stronger cocoon. The house, it appears, represented benign but ultimately distracting insulation from the strictures of the more immediate engagement with the world he found "up there" in concentration. The house's amenable comforts were seemingly gained only at the expense of experiential resonance, whereas the physical size of the hut necessarily intensified the interaction of individuals' "dwelling" with "places" of inhabitation, and its lack of building services demanded more active participation in obtaining the basic necessities. More comfortable, more public, closer to human affairs, the house could never be, for him, as acute a measure as the hut. It was not elementary enough, clouding rather than emphasizing questions of being.

Heidegger's hut and house can be seen as mirrors held up to the philosopher's life, reflecting different attitudes. One possible interpretation follows. The attitude reported by the hut can be aligned—broadly—with that of Heidegger's writings on "dwelling" and "place," with a living and making in which the small places of life and the activities that they support are deeply entwined. In this interpretation, the hut appears to stand for the philosophy of the engaged observer. Alongside this, the disposition suggested by the suburban house can be perceived as somewhat alien to Heidegger's writing, more aesthetic than "phenomenological," more attentive to the visual qualities of furniture and axial views than to emotion and experience. Its attitude can be found rooted in suburban affectation and bound more deeply with conventional social and domestic proprieties, more complicit with technological comforts and their influence on immediate experience of the world. Of the two attitudes of this interpretation, that reported by the house can be perceived as the setting of a suburban patriarch and his family: civic and somewhat affected, admitting a measure of hubris. This state of mind might somehow throw into sharp relief an alternative suggested by the hut, which could be perceived as solitary by preference, more attuned to emotion and experience.

However, the situation is more complex than this interpretation allows. While Heidegger eulogized the rigor of hut life in "Why Do I Stay in the Provinces?" and mythologized its perceived virtues by association with the *Schwarzwaldhof* of "Building Dwelling Thinking," it seems he made only passing contact with the engaged order that he wrote about. It was a world that persisted for him in solitary fragments. Alongside was another life always in attendance, that of the institutional academic. The philosopher was not a full-time resident of the hut, but always also based in Marburg or Freiburg. Indeed, the hut's upkeep depended on Heidegger's salary from the university. The priorities of this other life intervened at Todtnauberg: Digne Meller-Marcovicz's photographs show aspects of suburban domesticity enacted there; he wrote in awareness of the wider implications of his texts and their reception; and, most surprisingly, he later allowed the building to be equipped with electric light and a telephone. Heidegger sought his preferred order in the mountains at every opportunity, but it was never more than transitory. While—partly by choice and partly by compulsion—he found himself at increasing distance from the priorities of the academy, growing closer to his mountain home, he maintained city and provincial lives in parallel. The hut manifests this continuing tension: it appears at one with the landscape; its study, kitchen, and dining area have the compressed utility of a place where life is lived intensely; yet always apparent are the shutters and bars, provisions made for the building to be locked up and left behind (fig. 52).

The house on Rötebuckweg is also a little more complex than it first appears. The suburban aspiration of *rus in urbe*—a romance of country life recreated in a circumscribed city enclave—is by no means unique to Heidegger and his family. Thus manifested, the suburban ideal is easily criticized as neither one outlook nor another, naively utopian, blandly combining the worst of city and country with few of the benefits of either. Such charges can be leveled at the philosopher's house, and he seems to have come to acknowledge them through his own lack of enthusiasm for life there. Yet Heidegger's complicity with suburbia is evident, not least in beginning to suburbanize his hut with electricity. The aestheticized domesticity of Heidegger's house has already been discussed as bound into social aspiration, exemplified by its composition around visitors' impressions, the display of fine furniture, and the architectural delineation of traditional family roles. Considered in the scheme of Heidegger's engaged philosophy of "dwelling" and "place," such gestures seem to ring hollow. However, the Black Forest shingle hanging, while it can be perceived as suburban posturing, might also be interpreted as a reminder of a hut life always there in parallel. The garden terrace central to the ground floor plan, focused on the distant view—described by Elfride Heidegger as the summertime center of family life—provided a much-used outdoor room that might also be interpreted as an echo of the hut and its distinctive engagement between inside and outside.

Remembering these complexities, it is possible to consider the hut and house as talismanic for two positions decisive in Heidegger's biography, which Albert Borgmann terms "provincialism" and "cosmopolitanism."[87] These positions are often considered in opposition. Tropes recur by which advocates of each position attempt to dismiss the alternative. Cosmopolitans dismiss the provincial as invidious: introvert, inbred, prone to exclusion, and reliant upon romantic myth.[88] Provincials dismiss the cosmopolitan as

52. Although the hut seems to be somewhere life is lived intensely, always apparent are the shutters and bars, provisions made for the building to be locked up and left behind.

deluded: bound up in abstract systems and priorities, entranced by the fickleness of fashion, setting itself and its self-appointed heroes on false pedestals.[89] Although such polarities are inevitably caricatures, and provincial and cosmopolitan positions always remain more nuanced, their identification can be helpful. Borgmann characterizes four phases of Heidegger's life in terms of the provincial and cosmopolitan: first, the philosopher's early life emerging from the provincialism of Meßkirch; second, the start of his university career leading to the formulation of *Being and Time,* a quest to spar with the elite which he calls a "radical metacosmopolitanism"; third, a crisis of his philosophy, culminating in his failed rectorship, railing against a perceived futility of practical and constructive cosmopolitanism; and, fourth, a final articulation of a critical and affirmative provincialism beginning with the *Contributions to Philosophy.*[90] However, although the house and hut might be useful markers for specific dispositions, the house does not quite illustrate a neat cosmopolitanism and by no means does the hut illustrate a neat provincialism. Attitudes reflected by Heidegger's house and hut question such clear-cut distinctions, suggesting a continuing and complex tension between the provincial and cosmopolitan throughout the philosopher's mature life and work.

Heidegger's own critique of the Black Forest farmhouse myth is echoed here. He argued that the provincialism of the *Schwarzwaldhof* belonged to a lost era, its surface covered over by concerns of cosmopolitanism. Although he found important lessons in his perception of an old order of mountain life, the engaged rigor he found in it was, for him, no longer attainable in its former guise. He sought new affirmations of its character. Likewise, it appears that only through intimate retreat at the hut did Heidegger feel he could reach out, beyond cosmopolitan priorities, to the echoes of this particular provincialism; and he perceived that Freiburg, insulated by the cocoon of modern comforts, left him all but deaf to it. However, it is important that his provincialism and cosmopolitanism were always there together, mediating each other and subsisting on their mutual tensions.

Charges of invidiousness may always attend any romance of a lost provincialism supposedly free from cosmopolitan delusions. Where some sort of authentic rootedness is claimed, must there not be outsiders inevitably doomed to inauthenticity? Where toughness and rigor are sought, might intolerance be encouraged? Is hostility to the fashions of cultural debate the beginning of a dangerous totalitarianism? Where the transcendence of "nature" is evoked, might it not allow an unhealthy detachment from human responsibility? Moreover, might not biological determinism and the rhetoric of blood and soil follow close behind? While any provincialism invites such questions, because of Heidegger's involvement with Nazism they haunt in a special way both his writings on dwelling and place and any appreciation of the hut at Todtnauberg. It has been argued that the philosophy that he claimed from the mountains, freighted with Hölderlinian providence and arguably imagined as a recovery of pre-Socratic Greece, predisposed Heidegger to the barbaric ideology of Nazism.[91] In this context, as noted above with respect to Paul Celan, many have speculated on whether his thinking must necessarily remain upon German ground or whether it has wider reach. Heidegger's biography brings the cloud of fascism lower over provincialism, asking forcefully whether it must always be invidious and authoritarian.

It is not the aim of this short biographical book to address this philosophical question, although there may be insights here that help to illuminate it. Approaches to this question will inevitably color present-day interpretations of Heidegger's hut at Todtnauberg. Deeply bound into the philosopher's spiritual landscape, the building and its setting will be perceived by his advocates in the terms of his writing; for devotees it may even be a site of pilgrimage. Some, conscious of Celan's writing, will have a more guarded interest in heights which must always remain distant. More forthright critics will find the hut a suspicious and objectionable place, seeing continued interest in it only as grim fascination. Others will perceive an unremarkable building in a remarkable landscape, once occupied by the very human couple seen in Meller-Marcovicz's photographs. There are many possibilities.

Any interpretation must also be colored by the Heidegger family's recent embrace of tourism. The "Martin Heidegger Rundweg" (Martin Heidegger Trail), a three-kilometer waymarked walk, was laid out around the valley in 2002 (fig. 53). Heidegger was himself scathing of escapism, writing sarcastically about the stimulation of a "city-dweller" by "a so-called 'stay in the country'" in "Why Do I Stay in the Provinces?" The making of this

path, accompanied by five large signs presenting images and text about the philosopher's biography, is important. Some will feel that it has little bearing on the hut and its landscape, and view it as a mere practicality for a family in search of privacy. Others, however, may perceive it as a commodification of Heidegger's "work-world." The tourist signs might suggest that the hut at Todtnauberg has now joined the philosopher's conjectural *Schwarzwaldhof* in the realm of romantic myth. In another interpretation, one could argue that they indicate Heidegger's hut life was never indistinguishable from the escapist project, his time at Todtnauberg never more meaningful than the indulgence of a bourgeois romance. The arrival of organized tourism must inevitably make the hut's interpretation more complex.

In architecture, "sustainable" thinking has been linked with Heidegger's work on dwelling and place.[92] Such thinking seems cautious of technology. It promotes a caring attitude to "the environment," a passive approach to energy use and building services, the specification of "low-impact" materials, and recycling of building fabric and resources. It also promotes the local alongside the global, seeking meaning and

53. A sign near Todtnauberg Youth Hostel marking the start and finish of the Heidegger tourist trail.

belonging in "sustainable communities." Accompanied by predictions of catastrophe and statistical quantifications, such notions offer a damning critique of Western consumption and a compelling stimulus to action. However, complexities associated with the philosophy of Heidegger's hut appear relevant. "Sustainability" is often argued in the vocabulary of authenticity, "nature" valorized over the human. "Sustainable technology"—sometimes manifest in the development of energy-consuming devices for reducing the energy consumption of other devices—is seldom perceived as a contradiction in terms. The localism of sustainability is as plugged in to networks and logistics of technological society as it is rooted in neighborhood gardens and allotments. Relations between provincialism and cosmopolitanism are as contested here as they are with respect to Heidegger and his hut—a comparison addressed by Elfride Jelinek, who has parodied a present-day young *Mutter* concerned with "nature" and organic food in satirized Heideggerian dialogue.[93] Questions of technology, authenticity, and agency seem paramount to sustainability and the terms in which it is couched: critical attention is required.

For architecture, Heidegger's hut-inspired thinking about dwelling and place seems to have become a zero-sum game: whatever it gives, its associations can also take away. However, if Heidegger's hut might make a contribution, it appears to lie in the memory of its centering power for the philosopher's life.[94] The small building was the philosopher's datum, its particularities delineating the particularities of his life and work. Arguably, the greatest potential of the hut lies in the hope that such centering power need not be invidious or exclusive. Why cannot every life hold out hope for a resonant, centering datum? This need not keep others at bay, cast them as strangers, or be situated outside the city. The hut's memory suggests strategies for making such a datum. It might frame in rich and multiple ways itself, its inhabitants and their relationships, its equipment, its social context, the theater of passersby, the sun and tracking shadows, glimpses of the sky, breeze and wind, rain and snow, flora and fauna. It might be neither too big nor unnecessarily flexible, instead helping its occupants to configure intensities of situation. It might encourage reflective moments thought at a slower pace. Configuring daily, weekly, and seasonal routines, such a datum could dignify and sustain any life, attuned to the commonplace closely watched. Such centering may arguably be achieved more easily in a rural setting. However, the challenge posed by the hut's memory, particularly for architects, is how so powerful a datum might be achieved—without exclusion—in urban conditions.

It is clear that the hut and its surroundings offered Heidegger things and events that, for him, prompted reflection and stimulated contemplation. Todtnauberg intensified his experiences and conditioned his emotive inclinations. The situation reports moments of intimate intensity that the philosopher felt in his contemplations. The building stands for Heidegger's physical and textual presence. Reflected in it, and its landscape, are some of Heidegger's remarks, his sense of his own existence, and conceptual elements structuring his thought.

NOTES

Prologue

1.   The fragment in question can be found in C. Kahn, *The Art and Thought of Heraclitus* (Cambridge: Cambridge University Press, 1979), p. 43.

2.   The evocation of the everyday is deliberate. This is, after all, a key term in *Being and Time*. For Heidegger, what was important was to exert mastery over the everyday: "In everydayness Dasein can undergo a dull 'suffering', sink away in the dullness of it, and evade it by seeking new ways in which its dispersion in its affairs may be further dispersed. In the moment of vision and often just for that moment of vision, existence can gain mastery over the everyday; but it can never extinguish it." (M. Heidegger, *Being and Time*, trans. J. Macquarrie and E. Robinson [Oxford: Basil Blackwell, 1978], p. 371.)

3.   W. Benjamin, "One Way Street," in *Walter Benjamin: Selected Writings*, vol. 1 (Cambridge: Harvard University Press, 2003), p. 213.

4.   See in particular Heidegger, *Being and Time*, pp. 95–122.

5.   On *Gelassenheit* see Heidegger, *Discourse on Thinking*, trans. J. M. Anderson and E. H. Freund (New York: Harper & Row, 1966).

6.   Heidegger, *Being and Time*, p. 236.

Heidegger's Hut

1.   M. Heidegger, "Why Do I Stay in the Provinces?," trans. T. Sheehan, in T. Sheehan, ed., *Heidegger: The Man and the Thinker* (Chicago: Precedent, 1981).

2.   Ibid., p. 28.

3.   Ibid.

4.   H. Ott, *Martin Heidegger: A Political Life,* trans. A. Blunden (London: Fontana, 1994), pp. 41–58; R. Safranski, *Martin Heidegger: Between Good and Evil,* trans. E. Osers (Cambridge, MA: Harvard University Press, 1998), pp. 1–15.

5.   Heidegger was a Jesuit novitiate for only two weeks, discharged on the grounds of ill health. Ott, *Martin Heidegger: A Political Life,* pp. 64–89.

6.   Ibid., pp. 172–186.

7.   Many texts address this question, including J. Collins, *Heidegger and the Nazis* (Cambridge: Icon, 2000); V. Farías, *Heidegger and Nazism* (Philadelphia: Temple University Press, 1989); T. Kisiel, "Heidegger's Apology: Biography as Philosophy and Ideology," *Graduate Faculty Philosophy Journal,* 14:2–15:1 (1991), 363–404; J.-F. Lyotard, *Heidegger and the jews* [sic], trans. A. Michael and M. Roberts (Minneapolis: University of Minnesota Press, 1990); A. Milchman and A. Rosenberg, eds., *Martin Heidegger and the Holocaust* (Atlantic Highlands, NJ: Humanities Press International, 1996); G. Neske and E. Kettering, eds., *Martin Heidegger and National Socialism: Questions and Answers,* trans. L. Harries (New York: Paragon House, 1990); Ott, *Martin Heidegger: A Political Life;* T. Rockmore and J. Margolis, *The Heidegger Case: On Philosophy and Politics* (Philadelphia: Temple University Press, 1992); Safranski, *Martin Heidegger: Between Good and Evil.*

8.   Ott, *Martin Heidegger: A Political Life,* pp. 140–148.

9.   Heidegger's rectoral address has been translated as: M. Heidegger, "The Rectorate 1933/34: Facts and Thoughts," trans. K. Harries, *Review of Metaphysics* 38 (1985), 481–502.

10. Ott, *Martin Heidegger: A Political Life*, pp. 263–307.

11. M. Heidegger, *Contributions to Philosophy (From Enowning)*, trans. P. Emad and K. Maly (Bloomington: Indiana University Press, 1999).

12. Heidegger's apologia was published posthumously: M. Heidegger, *Die Selbstbehauptung der deutschen Universität—Das Rektorat 1933/34, Tatsachen und Gedanken* (Frankfurt: Vittorio Klostermann, 1983); in English as Heidegger, "The Rectorate 1933/34: Facts and Thoughts," trans. K. Harries.

13. The judgment is summarized, and a decisive report by Karl Jaspers to the Freiburg "de-Nazification" committee is quoted at length, in Ott, *Martin Heidegger: A Political Life*, pp. 309–351.

14. Ibid., pp. 359–368; H. W. Petzet, *Encounters and Dialogues with Martin Heidegger*, trans. P. Emad and K. Maly (Chicago: University of Chicago Press, 1993), pp. 68–75.

15. Patterns of alignment between these priorities have been traced in a case study of the Pfalz region in C. Applegate, *A Nation of Provincials: The German Idea of Heimat* (Berkeley: University of California Press, 1990).

16. D. Blackbourn and G. Eley, *The Peculiarities of German History* (Oxford: Oxford University Press), 1984. Parameters of the *Sonderweg* debate—as much constitutional, political, and economic as intellectual—are outlined on pp. 1–35.

17. Kisiel, "Heidegger's Apology," pp. 363–404.

18. M. Heidegger, "Building Dwelling Thinking," trans. A. Hofstadter, in *Martin Heidegger: Basic Writings*, ed. D. Farrell-Krell (London: Routledge, 1993), pp. 347–363; M. Heidegger, ". . . Poetically, Man Dwells . . . ," in *Poetry, Language, Thought*, trans. A. Hofstadter (New York: Harper and Row, 1971), pp. 211–229.

19. C. Norberg-Schulz, *Architecture, Meaning and Place: Selected Essays* (New York: Rizzoli, 1988); C. Norberg-Schulz, "Heidegger's Thinking on Architecture," in K. Nesbitt,

ed., *Theorizing a New Agenda for Architecture: An Anthology of Architectural Theory 1965–1995* (New York: Princeton Architectural Press, 1996), pp. 429–439; K. Frampton, "On Reading Heidegger," in Nesbitt, ed., *Theorizing a New Agenda for Architecture,* pp. 440–446; D. Vesely, *Architecture in the Age of Divided Representation: The Question of Creativity in the Shadow of Production* (Cambridge, MA: MIT Press, 2004); A. Pérez-Gómez, *Architecture and the Crisis of Modern Science* (Cambridge, MA: MIT Press, 1983); A. Pérez-Gómez, "Dwelling on Heidegger: Architecture as Mimetic Techno-Poiesis," *Cloud Cuckoo Land: International Journal of Architectural Theory* 2 (1998) at http://www.theo.tu-cottbus.de/Wolke/eng/Impress/impressum.html (10 October 1998); P. Blundell-Jones, *Hans Scharoun* (London: Phaidon, 1995); C. Alexander, *The Timeless Way of Building* (Oxford: Oxford University Press, 1977); S. Grabow, *Christopher Alexander and the Search for a New Paradigm in Architecture* (Stocksfield: Oriel Press, 1983); C. St. John Wilson, *The Other Tradition of Modern Architecture: The Uncompleted Project* (London: Academy, 1995); S. Holl, J. Pallasmaa, and A. Pérez-Gómez, "Questions of Perception: Phenomenology of Architecture," *A+U* special issue 7 (1994); P. Zumthor and H. Binet, *Peter Zumthor Works: Buildings and Projects 1979–1997* (Baden: Lars Müller, 1998); P. Zumthor, "A Way of Looking at Things," *A+U* special issue 2 (1998), 6–24.

20.   "Nur noch ein gott kann uns retten," *Der Spiegel* 23 (1976), 193–219; translated as "Only a God Can Save Us," trans. W. J. Richardson, in Sheehan, ed., *Heidegger: The Man and the Thinker,* pp. 45–67.

21.   For example, Heinrich Wiegand Petzet, effectively Heidegger's approved biographer, wrote in the 1980s: "The usual path, which led from the youth hostel of Todtnauberg to the hut . . . took almost an hour." Petzet, *Encounters and Dialogues,* p. 195. The walk takes ten to fifteen minutes in good weather.

22.   This is asserted by Petzet in *Encounters and Dialogues,* p. 192. However, a sign recently erected for tourists above Heidegger's hut claims that electricity was installed in 1931.

23.   Ibid., p. 201.Petzet interprets Heidegger's relationship with Hebel: M. Heidegger, "Hebel—Friend of the House," trans. B. V. Foltz and M. Heim, in D. E. Christensen,

M. Ridel, R. Spaemann, et al., eds., *Contemporary German Philosophy*, vol. 3 (University Park: Pennsylvania State University Press, 1983), pp. 89–101.

24. Hugo Ott describes at length the circumstances surrounding this appointment: see Ott, *Martin Heidegger: A Political Life*, pp. 122–129. Although the appointment was not confirmed formally until December 1922, it seems that there were very positive informal indications by the summer of 1922. Heidegger was also under consideration for a chair at Göttingen at this time.

25. Safranski, *Martin Heidegger: Between Good and Evil*, pp. 276–280. Heidegger refers to his relationship with the region of his birth in M. Heidegger, "The Pathway," trans. T. F. O'Meara and T. Sheehan, in Sheehan, ed., *Heidegger: The Man and the Thinker*, pp. 69–71.

26. "Was it the slopes, which in winter were covered with deep snow, that initially attracted Heidegger the avid skier? Or was it the magnificent solitude, pregnant with thought, that drew him there . . . that simple, ascetic place for thinking—a place that provided him with the breathing space he needed." Petzet, *Encounters and Dialogues*, p. 192. "The building of . . . Todtnauberg . . . was also in the service of this creative [philosophical] work. For it was in the stillness of the Black Forest that he worked with utmost concentration, and it was here that the lectures and lessons were prepared and the works written, the impact of which is felt throughout the world." W. Biemel, *Martin Heidegger: An Illustrated Study*, trans. J. L. Mehta (New York: Harcourt Brace, 1976), p. xii.

27. He appears to have empathized with a tradition of such philosopher's huts: see Petzet, *Encounters and Dialogues*, p. 217.

28. Heidegger, "The Pathway," pp. 69–71; Ott, *Martin Heidegger: A Political Life*, pp. 41–58.

29. Heidegger, letters to Karl Jaspers dated 29 April and 4 October 1926, in *Martin Heidegger & Karl Jaspers: Briefwechsel*, ed. Biemel and Saner, cited in Ott, *Martin Heidegger: A Political Life*, p. 125.

30.   Heidegger, "The Pathway," pp. 69–71.

31.   The location of the picture matches the landscape not far from the hut, just above Todtnauberg Youth Hostel.

32.   Heidegger lectured on skiing on at least one occasion: K. Löwith, *My Life in Germany before and after 1933: A Report*, trans. E. King (London: Athlone, 1994), p. 33. Heinrich Heidegger reports that his uncle was a strict ski teacher—"no lifts!"

33.   Text of a tourist sign written by Hermann Heidegger, the philosopher's son, erected near the hut in 2002.

34.   M. Heidegger, "The Thing," in *Poetry, Language, Thought*, pp. 163–186; T. Kisiel, *The Genesis of Heidegger's Being and Time* (Berkeley: University of California Press, 1993), pp. 309ff.

35.   Safranski, *Martin Heidegger: Between Good and Evil*, pp. 40–54. The author is also grateful to Hermann Heidegger for confirming this in a letter of January 2000.

36.   From the text of a tourist sign erected near the hut in 2002.

37.   One such occasion is described in Ott, *Martin Heidegger: A Political Life*, p. 224.

38.   Petzet, *Encounters and Dialogues*, pp. 197–198.

39.   W. Biemel, *Heidegger* (Hamburg: Rohwolt Taschenbuch Verlag, 1973), p. 36. This farmhouse, belonging to Johann Brender, has subsequently been demolished and no record of it has been traced. It is possible that Heidegger worked in this house before construction of the hut, which might have been a factor in his choice of Todtnauberg for construction of a retreat.

40.   Löwith, *My Life in Germany*, p. 32.

41.   Safranski, *Martin Heidegger: Between Good and Evil*, p. 132.

42.   Safranski writes: "This was intended to be a mixture of scout camp and Platonic academy. . . . Science was once more open to awaken 'the living reality of nature and of

history'; the 'sterile preoccupation with ideologies' of Christianity and 'positivist fact-mongering' were to be overcome. . . . It was realised from October 4 to 10, 1933, in a place below the Todtnauberg cabin. . . . Heidegger had selected a small circle of associate professors and students and drawn up the stage directions: 'The company will proceed to the destination on foot . . . SA or SS service uniform will be worn; the uniform of the Stahlhelm (with armband) may also be worn.' The daily roster began with reveille at 06:00 hours and ended with the tattoo at 22:00 hours. 'The real work of the camp will be to reflect on ways and means for fighting for the attainment of the University of the future for the German mind and spirit.' Heidegger wants to bring a group of young people to his peaceful Todtnauberg to build campfires, share food, sing along with guitar—but he announced the project as if it were a march into enemy country. . . . A certain note of unpleasantness was provided by a cabal between Heidegger's faithful followers and a group of SA brownshirt students from Heidelberg, who confronted the Youth League tradition with their own military spirit and championed a militant anti-Semitism. In his self-justification for the denazification procedure in 1945, Heidegger inflated this into a political conflict. . . . The powers of Dasein that are evidently involved here are of a men's club and scout variety. Heidegger, however, manages to set up a stage on which conspiracy, intrigue and intergroup tensions have the appearance of something 'great.'" Safranski, *Martin Heidegger: Between Good and Evil*, pp. 262–263.

43.   Heidegger, "The Rectorate 1933/34: Facts and Thoughts." Hugo Ott's discussion of the camp—in parts—contests Heidegger's account, based on correspondence between the philosopher and Rudolf Stadelmann, then a young lecturer at Freiburg University: Ott, *Martin Heidegger: A Political Life*, pp. 224–234.

44.   Petzet, *Encounters and Dialogues*, p. 194.

45.   Heidegger's manuscripts were typed by his brother Fritz in their town of birth, Meßkirch. Fritz Heidegger also stored the original scripts. Petzet, *Encounters and Dialogues*, p. 205.

46.   Ibid., p. 193.

47.   D. J. Constantine, *The Significance of Locality in the Poetry of Friedrich Hölderlin* (London: MHRA, 1979), p. 4.

48.   *Martin Heidegger & Karl Jaspers: Briefwechsel*, p. 53; quoted in Safranski, *Martin Heidegger: Between Good and Evil*, pp. 142–143.

49.   Heidegger, "Why Do I Stay in the Provinces?," pp. 27–28.

50.   Ott, *Martin Heidegger: A Political Life*, pp. 149–171.

51.   The philosopher's title intentionally avoided commas to emphasize a unity he perceived between the three notions. See A. Hofstadter, introduction to Heidegger, *Poetry, Language, Thought*, p. xiii.

52.   Heidegger, "Building Dwelling Thinking," pp. 361–362. I have slightly amended the translation.

53.   This building was subsequently destroyed by fire and replaced with a newer structure. It was built into the bank, adjacent to the stream that passes the hut, facing south, surveying the landscape and the valley floor. Heidegger worked at the Brender house over a number of years and was familiar with his landlord's family, their work, and the patterns of their lives. Involved with local forestry in his younger years, Heidegger would have been acquainted with a number of his neighbors and their lives at *Schwarzwaldhöfe* close to the hut.

54.   Heidegger, "The Thinker as Poet," in *Poetry, Language, Thought*, pp. 1–14.

55.   Hermann Heidegger, speaking in *Human, All too Human: Thinking the Unthinkable—Martin Heidegger*, BBC2 Television UK, Weatherview, 10 August 1999, 23:15.

56.   The German "der Guß" (libation) recurs in Heidegger's later writings where it refers to a drink "poured for the immortal gods." Heidegger, "The Thing," p. 172.

57.   A six-pointed star, the star of David, symbolizes the "wandering" people of Judaism. Heidegger claimed that his star also stood for the "wandering" thinker. A star

was also used as the motif atop his gravestone in Meßkirch (rather than a cross), although with five points rather than six. Whether there was any connection intended between the philosopher's star and the star of David is a contentious point given his political history, not least because the star represented victimhood in postwar Germany.

58.   Petzet, *Encounters and Dialogues*, p. 217.

59.   Ibid.

60.   A. Cline, *A Hut of One's Own: Life Outside the Circle of Architecture* (Cambridge, MA: MIT Press, 1997).

61.   R. May, *Heidegger's Hidden Sources: East Asian Influences on His Work*, ed. and trans. G. Parkes (London: Routledge, 1996), pp. 12, 60.

62.   H. D. Thoreau, *Walden* (London: Everyman's Library, Dent, 1968).

63.   Von Schonfeld et al., "The Vastness of All Grown Things: Martin Heidegger's Cabin at Todtnauberg and Ludwig Wittgenstein's Cabin at Skjølden," *Daidalos* 32 (1989), 84–87; F. Samuel, "A Confession of Faith in Stone: Carl Gustav Jung's Tower at Bollingen," *Things* 8 (1998), 49–60.

64.   Hannah Arendt (with whom Heidegger had an affair in the mid-1920s) wrote of the philosopher and his hut in 1949: "That life in Todtnauberg, this railing against civilisation, and writing Sein ['being'] with a y [the archaic form] is in reality a kind of mouse hole into which he withdrew. . . ." Quoted in E. Ettinger, *Hannah Arendt / Martin Heidegger* (New Haven: Yale University Press, 1995), p. 67.

65.   These names are listed by Petzet in *Encounters and Dialogues*, p. 192. The author has not had access to the visitors' book.

66.   Ibid., pp. 195–196.

67.   Kommerell appears to have misremembered the hut here. There are three windows in the dining area of the *Vorraum*.

68.   M. Kommerell, *Briefe und Aufzeichnungen 1919–1944: Aus dem Nachlaß*, ed. I. Jens (Freiburg am Breisgau and Konstanz: Olten, 1967), pp. 377–383. This English translation appears in Petzet, *Encounters and Dialogues*, pp. 193–195.

69.   G. Baumann, *Erinnerungen an Paul Celan* (Frankfurt: Suhrkamp, 1986), cited in J. Felsteiner, *Paul Celan: Poet, Survivor, Jew* (New Haven: Yale University Press, 1995), p. 245.

70.   Felsteiner, *Paul Celan*, p. 245.

71.   In the original version of this poem, which Celan sent to Heidegger in 1968, an additional bracketed line ("un/tarryingly coming") was added here. This was deleted for the published version in 1970. Refer to Safranski, *Martin Heidegger: Between Good and Evil*, p. 424.

72.   P. Celan, "Todtnauberg," in *Selected Poems*, trans. M. Hamburger (London: Penguin, 1996), p. 301. This volume also contains the German text of "Todtnauberg" as published in 1970.

73.   Felsteiner, *Paul Celan*, p. 246.

74.   These meanings are interpreted in almost word-for-word detail in O. Pöggler, "Todtnauberg," in Milchman and Rosenburg, eds., *Martin Heidegger and the Holocaust*, pp. 102–112.

75.   Ibid.

76.   Pöggler writes: "By this time had not everything to do with the land finally lost its innocence, insofar as remote locations were made to serve as concentration camps . . . for example . . . Heuberg or Kislau near Karlsruhe . . . ?" Ibid.

77.   Jelinek's play is a biting satire on Heidegger, his distinctive German language and its contemporary appropriations. Its title changes the name of the hut's location from Todtnauberg to Totenauberg, inserting the German word "tot" (dead). The drama is based on a fictionalized accusatory meeting between two characters representing

Heidegger and Hannah Arendt. E. Jelinek, *Totenauberg: Ein Stück* (Reinbek bei Hamburg: Rohwolt, 2004), translated as *Death/Valley/Summit (Totenauberg)*, trans. G. Honegger, in C. Weber, ed., *Drama Contemporary Germany* (Baltimore: Johns Hopkins University Press, 1996), pp. 217–264.

78.   This second house has been substantially altered and divided in two. Neither Heidegger's family nor Freiburg city authorities have any record of its original condition. Heinrich Wiegand Petzet wrote: "When Heidegger left this [the original Freiburg] house after his eightieth birthday and moved into a residence built for his old age on the lower edge of the garden, some of the Biedermeier pieces [of furniture] accompanied him. . . . The new [house] was basically like a tent; it was a last station in which the thinker was granted five more happy years to live. Practical considerations led to this decision, whose planning was . . . in Frau Heidegger's capable hands . . . this new residence had a spacious attic for housing the visiting friends and students from France . . . the walls of the study in the comfortable and simple little house at Fillibachstrasse 25 heard other significant conversations. It was in this house that Heidegger discussed the plan for the *Gesamtausgabe* for hours every week." Petzet, *Encounters and Dialogues,* p. 188.

79.   The house has been listed by city authorities because of its connection with the philosopher. The author is grateful to Herr Menzel of the *Regierungspräsidium* in Freiburg for providing copies of drawings, the listing description, and some comments on the house forwarded to them by Prof. Dr. Hugo Ott. I am also grateful to Gertrud Heidegger for the opportunity to visit the house.

80.   Heidegger cared little for his first professorial appointment at Marburg University, which he took up in 1923. Hugo Ott considers Heidegger's return to Freiburg as almost triumphal: "*Being and Time* appeared in the summer of 1927. The great breakthrough predicted by Husserl had finally come . . . it was only a matter of weeks before moves were afoot in Freiburg, at Husserl's instigation, to offer Heidegger the chair there. . . . Even before Heidegger had accepted the offer at Freiburg, the plot of land above Freiburg-Zähringen had been purchased, and the builders worked through the summer of 1928 to

get the house ready for occupation by the winter. The exile had returned." Ott, *Martin Heidegger: A Political Life*, pp. 106–129.

81.   It has been possible to trace only a little information about Fetter. City authorities were unable to provide any further information, as relevant professional records were destroyed in wartime and his name is not listed after 1945. His other projects included the cable car station above Freiburg.

82.   The term "Biedermeier" is equally applicable to literature and poetry. See H. Watanabe-O'Kelly, ed., *The Cambridge History of German Literature* (Cambridge: Cambridge University Press, 1997), pp. 272–326; M. J. Norst, "Biedermeier," in J. M. Ritchie, ed., *Periods in German Literature* (London: Oswald Wolff, 1966), pp. 147–170.

83.   The timber lintel above the door bears the painted inscription chosen by Heidegger. It is a German translation of Proverbs 4:23, which translates to English as "Shelter your heart with all vigilance; for from it flow the springs of life." Proverbs 4 concerns wisdom. Heidegger's opportune translation is one of a number of possible renderings of the original.

84.   Adalbert Stifter (1805–1868) was an Austrian-born author linked with the Biedermeier movement. His principal work, *Der Nachsommer* (the title can be translated as "Indian Summer"), has been found loquacious in its nostalgia, heavy with description and dialogue: see Watanabe-O'Kelly, ed., *The Cambridge History of German Literature,* pp. 299–301. Heidegger wrote a short essay about Stifter: M. Heidegger, "Adalbert Stifters 'Eisgeschichte,'" in *Aus der Erfahrung des Denkens 1910–1976* (Frankfurt: Vittorio Klostermann, 1983), pp. 185–198.

85.   Quoted in Petzet, *Encounters and Dialogues,* p. 186.

86.   R. Schürmann, "Reiner Schürmann's Report of His Visit to Martin Heidegger," trans. P. Adler, *Graduate Faculty Philosophy Journal* 19:2–20:1 (1997), 67–68.

87.   A. Borgmann, "Cosmopolitanism and Provincialism: On Heidegger's Errors and Insights," *Philosophy Today* 36 (Summer 1992), 131–145.

88.   There are a number of writers who have used this tack with respect to Heidegger's thinking: T. W. Adorno, *The Jargon of Authenticity,* trans. K. Tarnowski and F. Will (London: Routledge and Kegan Paul, 1986); J.-F. Lyotard, *Heidegger and the jews* [sic], trans. A. Michael and M. Roberts (Minneapolis: University of Minnesota Press, 1990); also, with respect to Heidegger's hut, N. Leach, "The Dark Side of the *Domus," Journal of Architecture* 3:1 (1998), 31–42; M. Wigley, "Heidegger's House: The Violence of the Domestic," *Columbia Documents of Architecture and Theory* 1 (1992), 91–121.

89.   Heidegger employs such arguments, for example, in "Why Do I Stay in the Provinces?," and in "The Question Concerning Technology," trans. W. Lovitt, in *Martin Heidegger: Basic Writings,* pp. 211–341.

90.   Borgmann, "Cosmopolitanism and Provincialism."

91.   K. Harries, *The Ethical Function of Architecture* (Cambridge, MA: MIT Press, 1997), p. 166.

92.   Such thinking is associated with debates in environmental ethics: see B. V. Foltz, "On Heidegger and the Interpretation of Environmental Crisis," *Environmental Ethics* 6 (1984); L. McWhorter, ed., *Heidegger and the Earth: Essays in Environmental Philosophy* (Kirksville, MI: Thomas Jefferson University Press, 1992).

93.   Jelinek, *Death/Valley/Summit,* pp. 232–243.

94.   Borgmann, "Cosmopolitanism and Provincialism," p. 140.

BIBLIOGRAPHY

Works by Martin Heidegger

"Adalbert Stifters '*Eisgeschichte*.'" In Heidegger, *Aus der Erfahrung des Denkens 1910–1976*. Frankfurt: Vittorio Klostermann, 1983, pp. 185–198.

Being and Time. Trans. J. Macquarrie and E. Robinson. New York: Harper and Row, 1962. [An alternative translation is available: *Being and Time*, trans. J. Stambaugh (Albany: State University of New York Press, 1996). First published as *Sein und Zeit* (Halle: Jahrbuch für Philosophie und phänomenologische Forschung, 1927). Commonly available in German as *Sein und Zeit*, ed. F.-W. von Hermann (Frankfurt: Vittorio Klostermann, 1977).]

"Building Dwelling Thinking." In Heidegger, *Poetry, Language, Thought*, trans. A. Hofstadter. New York: Harper and Row, 1971, pp. 143–161. Reprinted in *Martin Heidegger: Basic Writings*, ed. D. Farrell-Krell (London: Routledge, 1993), pp. 347–363. [The original German text has been published as "Bauen Wohnen Denken," in *Mensch und Raum: Das Darmstädter Gespräch 1951* (Braunschweig: Vieweg, 1991), pp. 88–102. More commonly available as "Bauen Wohnen Denken," in *Vorträge und Aufsätze* (Pfullingen: Neske, 1997), pp. 139–156.]

Contributions to Philosophy (From Enowning). Trans. P. Emad and K. Maly. Bloomington: Indiana University Press, 1999. [First published as *Beiträge zur Philosophie (Vom Ereignis)* (Frankfurt: Vittorio Klostermann, 1994).]

"Hebel—Friend of the House." Trans. B. V. Foltz and M. Heim. In D. E. Christensen, M. Ridel, R. Spaemann, et al., eds., *Contemporary German Philosophy*, vol. 3. University Park: Pennsylvania State University Press, 1983, pp. 89–100. [In German as *Hebel— das Hausfreund* (Pfullingen: Neske, 1957).]

"The Pathway." Trans. T. F. O'Meara and T. Sheehan. In T. Sheehan, ed., *Heidegger: The Man and the Thinker*. Chicago: Precedent, 1981, pp. 69–71. [In German as *Der Feldweg* (Frankfurt: Vittorio Klostermann, 1989).]

". . . Poetically, Man Dwells. . . ." In Heidegger, *Poetry, Language, Thought*, trans. A. Hofstadter. New York: Harper and Row, 1971, pp. 211–229. [First published as ". . . dichterisch wohnet der Mensch . . . ," *Akzente: Zeitschrift für Dichtung* 1 (1954), 57ff. Commonly available in German as ". . . dichterisch wohnet der Mensch . . . ," in *Vorträge und Aufsätze* (Pfullingen: Neske, 1997), pp. 181–198.]

Poetry, Language, Thought. Trans. A. Hofstadter. New York: Harper and Row, 1971.

"The Question Concerning Technology." Trans. W. Lovitt. In *Martin Heidegger: Basic Writings*, ed. D. Farrell-Krell. London: Routledge, 1993, pp. 211–341. [In German as "Die Frage nach der Technik," in *Vorträge und Aufsätze* (Pfullingen: Neske, 1954), pp. 9–40.]

"The Rectorate 1933/34: Facts and Thoughts." Trans. K. Harries. In *Review of Metaphysics* 38 (1985), 481–502. [In German as *Die Selbstbehauptung der deutschen Universität—Das Rektorat 1933/34, Tatsachen und Gedanken* (Frankfurt: Vittorio Klostermann, 1983).]

"The Thing." In Heidegger, *Poetry, Language, Thought*, trans. A. Hofstadter. New York: Harper and Row, 1971, pp. 163–186. [First published as "Das Ding," in *Jahrbuch der Akademie: Gestalt und Gedanke*, vol. 1, ed. C. Podewils (Munich: Bayerische Akademie der schönen Künste, 1951), pp. 128ff. Commonly available in German as "Das Ding," in *Vorträge und Aufsätze* (Pfullingen: Neske, 1997), pp. 157–179.]

"The Thinker as Poet." In Heidegger, *Poetry, Language, Thought,* trans. A. Hofstadter. New York: Harper and Row, 1971, pp. 1–14. [In German as M. Heidegger, *Aus der Erfahrung des Denkens* (Stuttgart: Neske, 1996).]

"Why Do I Stay in the Provinces?" Trans. T. Sheehan. In T. Sheehan, ed., *Heidegger: The Man and the Thinker.* Chicago: Precedent, 1981, pp. 27–28. [First published as "Warum bleiben wir in der Provinz?," in *Der Alemanne,* 7 March 1934. Commonly available in German as "Warum bleiben wir in der Provinz?," in *Nachlese zu Heidegger: Dokumente zu seinem Leben und Denken,* ed. G. Schneeberger (Bern: n.p., 1972), pp. 216–218.]

Heidegger's Correspondence

Briefe 1925 bis 1975, und andere Zeugnisse: Hannah Arendt und Martin Heidegger. Ed. A. Lutz. Frankfurt: Vittorio Klostermann, 1998.

Martin Heidegger & Elisabeth Blochmann: Briefwechsel. Ed. J. W. Storck. Marbach: Deutsches Schillergesellschaft, 1990.

Martin Heidegger & Erhart Kästner: Briefwechsel. Ed. H. W. Petzet. Frankfurt: Insel, 1986.

Martin Heidegger & Karl Jaspers: Briefwechsel. Ed. W. Biemel and H. Saner. Frankfurt: Vittorio Klostermann, 1990.

Other Works

Adorno, T. *The Jargon of Authenticity.* Trans. K. Tarnowski and F. Will. London: Routledge and Kegan Paul, 1986.

Applegate, C. *A Nation of Provincials: The German Idea of Heimat.* Berkeley: University of California Press, 1990.

Arendt, H. "Martin Heidegger at Eighty." *New York Review of Books,* 21 October 1971.

Augé, M. *Non-Places: Introduction to an Anthropology of Supermodernity.* London: Verso, 1995.

Ballantyne, A. "In a Dark Wood: Dwelling as Spatial Practice." *arq (Architectural Research Quarterly)* 4:4 (2000), 349–355.

Biemel, W. *Heidegger.* Hamburg: Rohwolt Taschenbuch Verlag, 1973.

Biemel, W. *Martin Heidegger: An Illustrated Study.* Trans. J. L. Mehta. New York: Harcourt Brace, 1976.

Blackbourn, D., and G. Eley. *The Peculiarities of German History.* Oxford: Oxford University Press, 1984.

Borgmann, A. "Cosmopolitanism and Provincialism: On Heidegger's Errors and Insights." *Philosophy Today* 36 (Summer 1992), 131–145.

Casey, E. *The Fate of Place: A Philosophical History.* Berkeley: University of California Press, 1997.

Celan, P. *Selected Poems.* Trans. M. Hamburger. London: Penguin, 1996.

Cline, A. *A Hut of One's Own: Life Outside the Circle of Architecture.* Cambridge, MA: MIT Press, 1997.

Collins, J. *Heidegger and the Nazis.* Cambridge: Icon, 2000.

Commenge, B. "D'un chemin à l'autre: de Messkirch à Todtnauberg." *Infini* 53 (1996), 47–57.

Constantine, D. J. *The Significance of Locality in the Poetry of Friedrich Hölderlin.* London: MHRA, 1979.

Dreyfus, H., and M. Wrathall. *Heidegger Reexamined: Art, Poetry and Technology.* London: Routledge, 2002.

El-Bizri, N. "On *kai khōra:* Situating Heidegger between the *Sophist* and the *Timeaus.*" *Studia Phænomenologica* 4:1–2 (2004), 73–98.

Elden, S. "Heidegger's Hölderlin and the Importance of Place." *Journal of the British Society of Phenomenology* 30:3 (1999), 258–274.

Ettinger, E. *Hannah Arendt / Martin Heidegger.* New Haven: Yale University Press, 1995.

Farías, V. *Heidegger and Nazism.* Philadelphia: Temple University Press, 1989.

Fedier, F. *Soixante-deux photographies de Martin Heidegger.* Gallimard: L'Infini, 2000.

Felsteiner, J. *Paul Celan: Poet, Survivor, Jew.* New Haven: Yale University Press, 1995.

Foltz, B. V. "On Heidegger and the Interpretation of Environmental Crisis." *Environmental Ethics* 6 (1984).

Frampton, K. "On Reading Heidegger." In K. Nesbitt, ed., *Theorizing a New Agenda for Architecture: An Anthology of Architectural Theory 1965–1995.* New York: Princeton Architectural Press, 1996, pp. 440–446.

Führ, E., ed. *Bauen und Wohnen: Martin Heideggers Grundlegung einer Phänomenologie der Architektur: Theoretische Untersuchungen zur Architektur 3.* Berlin: Waxmann Münster, 2000.

Gadamer, H.-G. *Heidegger's Ways.* Trans. J. W. Stanley. Albany: State University of New York Press, 1994.

Golb, J. B. "Celan and Heidegger: A Reading of Todtnauberg." *Seminar: A Journal of Germanic Studies* 24:3 (1990), 255–268.

Harries, K. *The Ethical Function of Architecture.* Cambridge, MA: MIT Press, 1997.

Heaney, S. "A Sense of Place." In *Preoccupations: Selected Prose 1968–1978.* London: Faber and Faber, 1980.

Heynen, H. "Worthy of Question: Heidegger's Role in Architectural Theory." *Archis* 12 (1993), 42–49.

Hölderlin, F. *Friedrich Hölderlin: Selected Poems and Fragments.* Trans. M. Hamburger. London: Penguin, 1998.

Holl, S., J. Pallasmaa, and A. Pérez-Gómez. "Questions of Perception: Phenomenology of Architecture." *A+U* special issue 7 (1994).

Human, All Too Human: Thinking the Unthinkable—Martin Heidegger. BBC2, Weatherview, 10 August 1999, 23:15.

Jelinek, E. *Totenauberg: Ein Stück.* Reinbek bei Hamburg: Rohwolt, 2004. [Translated as *Death/Valley/Summit (Totenauberg),* trans. G. Honegger, in C. Weber, ed., *Drama Contemporary Germany* (Baltimore: Johns Hopkins University Press, 1996), pp. 217–264.]

Kisiel, T. *The Genesis of Heidegger's Being and Time.* Berkeley: University of California Press, 1993.

Kisiel, T. "Heidegger's Apology: Biography as Philosophy and Ideology." *Graduate Faculty Philosophy Journal* 14:2 and 15:1 (1991), 363–404.

Kisiel, T. *Heidegger's Way of Thought: Critical and Interpretative Signposts.* Ed. A. Denker and M. Heinz. London: Continuum, 2002.

Kommerell, M. *Briefe und Aufzeichnungen 1919–1944: Aus dem Nachlaß.* Ed. I. Jens. Freiburg-im-Breisgau and Konstanz: Olten, 1967.

Leach, N. "The Dark Side of the *Domus.*" *Journal of Architecture* 3:1 (1998), 31–42.

Löwith, K. "Heidegger: A Thinker in Destitute Times." In Löwith, *Martin Heidegger and European Nihilism,* trans. G. Steiner, ed. R. Wolin. New York: Columbia University Press, 1995, pp. 29–134.

Löwith, K. *My Life in Germany before and after 1933: A Report.* Trans. E. King. London: Athlone, 1994.

Lyotard, J.-F. "*Domus* and the Megalopolis." In *The Inhuman,* trans. G. Bennington and R. Bowlby. Cambridge: Polity Press, 1991, pp. 191–204.

Lyotard, J.-F. *Heidegger and the jews* [sic]. Trans. A. Michael and M. Roberts. Minneapolis: University of Minnesota Press, 1990.

May, R. *Heidegger's Hidden Sources: East Asian Influences on His Work.* Ed. and trans. G. Parkes. London: Routledge, 1996.

McWhorter, L., ed. *Heidegger and the Earth: Essays in Environmental Philosophy.* Kirksville, MI: Thomas Jefferson University Press, 1992.

Meller-Marcovicz, D. *Martin Heidegger, Photos 23 September 1966 / 17+18 Juni 1968.* Frankfurt: Vittorio Klostermann, 1985.

Milchman, A., and A. Rosenberg, eds. *Martin Heidegger and the Holocaust.* Atlantic Highlands, NJ: Humanities Press International, 1996.

Neske, G., and E. Kettering, eds. *Martin Heidegger and National Socialism: Questions and Answers.* Trans. L. Harries. New York: Paragon House, 1990.

Norberg-Schulz, C. *Architecture, Meaning and Place: Selected Essays.* New York: Rizzoli, 1988.

Norberg-Schulz, C. "Heidegger's Thinking on Architecture." In K. Nesbitt, ed., *Theorizing a New Agenda for Architecture: An Anthology of Architectural Theory 1965–1995.* New York: Princeton Architectural Press, 1996, pp. 429–439.

Norst, M. J. "Biedermeier." In J. M. Ritchie, ed., *Periods in German Literature.* London: Oswald Wolff, 1966, pp. 147–170.

Ott, H. *Martin Heidegger: A Political Life.* Trans. A. Blunden. London: Fontana, 1994.

Pérez-Gómez, A. "Dwelling on Heidegger: Architecture as Mimetic Techno-Poiesis." *Cloud Cuckoo Land: International Journal of Architectural Theory* 2 (1998), at http://www.theo.tu-cottbus.de/Wolke/eng/Impress/impressum.html (10 October 1998).

Petzet, H. W. *Encounters and Dialogues with Martin Heidegger.* Trans. P. Emad and K. Maly. Chicago: University of Chicago Press, 1993.

Pöggler, O. *Martin Heidegger's Path of Thinking.* Trans. D. Magurshak and S. Barber. Atlantic Highlands, NJ: Humanities Press International, 1987.

Pöggler, O. "Todtnauberg." In A. Milchman and A. Rosenberg, eds., *Martin Heidegger and the Holocaust.* Atlantic Highlands, NJ: Humanities Press International, 1996, pp. 102–110.

Rabinbach, A. *In the Shadow of Catastrophe: German Intellectuals between Apocalypse and Enlightenment.* Berkeley: University of California Press, 1997.

Rockmore, T., and J. Margolis. *The Heidegger Case: On Philosophy and Politics.* Philadelphia: Temple University Press, 1992.

Safranski, R. *Martin Heidegger: Between Good and Evil.* Trans. E. Osers. Cambridge, MA: Harvard University Press, 1998.

Samuel, F. "A Confession of Faith in Stone: Carl Gustav Jung's Tower at Bollingen." *Things* 8 (1998), 49–60.

Schürmann, R. "Reiner Schürmann's Report of His Visit to Martin Heidegger." Trans. P. Adler. *Graduate Faculty Philosophy Journal* 19:2–20:1 (1997), 67–68.

Seamon, D. "Concretizing Heidegger's Notion of Dwelling: The Contributions of Thomas Thiis-Evensen and Christopher Alexander." *Cloud Cuckoo Land: International Journal of Architectural Theory* 2 (1998), at http://www.theo.tu-cottbus.de/Wolke/eng/Impress/impressum.html (10 October 1998).

Seamon, D., and R. Mugurauer, eds. *Dwelling, Place and Environment.* New York: Columbia University Press, 1989.

Sharr, A. "The Professor's House: Martin Heidegger's House at Freiburg-im-Breisgau." In S. Menin, ed., *Constructing Place.* London: Routledge, 2003.

Sharr, A., with S. Unwin. "Heidegger's Hut." *arq* (*Architectural Research Quarterly*) 5:1 (2001), 53–61.

Sheehan, T., ed. *Heidegger: The Man and the Thinker.* Chicago: Precedent, 1981.

Sluga, H. *Heidegger's Crisis: Philosophy and Politics in Nazi Germany.* Cambridge, MA: Harvard University Press, 1993.

Steiner, G. *Heidegger.* London: Fontana, 1992.

Thoreau, H. D. *Walden.* London: Everyman's Library, Dent, 1968.

Unwin, S. *Analysing Architecture.* London: Routledge, 2003.

Van Buren, J. *The Young Heidegger.* Bloomington: Indiana University Press, 1994.

Vesely, D. *Architecture in the Age of Divided Representation: The Question of Creativity in the Shadow of Production.* Cambridge, MA: MIT Press, 2004.

Von Schonfeld, R., et al. "The Vastness of All Grown Things: Martin Heidegger's Cabin at Todtnauberg and Ludwig Wittgenstein's Cabin at Skjølden." *Daidalos* 32 (1989), 84–87.

Watanabe-O'Kelly, H., ed. *The Cambridge History of German Literature.* Cambridge: Cambridge University Press, 1997.

Wigley, M. "Heidegger's House: The Violence of the Domestic." *Columbia Documents of Architecture and Theory* 1 (1992), 91–121.

Wilson, C. S. *The Other Tradition of Modern Architecture: The Uncompleted Project.* London: Academy, 1995.

Wolin, R., ed. *The Heidegger Controversy.* Cambridge, MA: MIT Press, 1993.

Young, J. *Heidegger, Philosophy, Nazism.* Cambridge: Cambridge University Press, 1997.

Young, J. *Heidegger's Later Philosophy.* Cambridge: Cambridge University Press, 2001.

Zumthor, P. *Thinking Architecture.* Baden: Lars Müller, 1998.

Zumthor, P., and H. Binet. *Peter Zumthor Works: Buildings and Projects 1979–1997.* Baden: Lars Müller, 1998.

INDEX